The GOLDEN AGE of ISLAM

What It Was And Why It Matters

"APPLE DIDN'T FALL ON NEWTON"

SALIM KHAN

White Falcon Publishing

The Golden Age of Islam
Salim Khan

Published by White Falcon Publishing
Chandigarh, India

The contents of this book have been certified and timestamped
on the Gnosis blockchain as a permanent proof of existence.
Scan the QR code or visit the URL given on the back cover
to verify the blockchain certification for this book.

ISBN - 978-93-34184-94-5

The
GOLDEN
AGE
of ISLAM

To My Mother. My Wife. My Daughter.

CONTENTS

PREFACE

Throughout history, some periods have been times of significant progress, creativity, and learning. The Golden Age of Islam began in the 8th century and stretched into the 13th century. During this time, the Islamic world became a cradle of knowledge and innovation, contributing profoundly to the sciences, arts, philosophy, aviation, history, geography and culture in ways that continue to shape our world today. The inspiration for this book stems from a deep admiration for the achievements of this era—a time when scholars, driven by a harmonious blend of faith and reason, pursued knowledge not only for its practical benefits but also as a divine calling.

This book explores and celebrates the legacy of those who lived during this transformative period, preserving and building upon the intellectual wealth of earlier civilisations while pioneering discoveries that would echo through the centuries (Sadly, to be forgotten).

The Golden Age of Islam was not merely a geographic or religious phenomenon. It was an era of collaboration across cultures, religions, and ethnicities. At its heart was the House of Wisdom in Baghdad, where scholars of diverse backgrounds worked side by side, translating Greek, Persian, and Indian texts into Arabic. This knowledge synthesis became a foundation upon which original ideas flourished, influencing fields as diverse as medicine, mathematics, astronomy, philosophy, history, geography, chemistry, cryptology, and the arts (Hard to believe we were such diverse, right?).

In these pages, you will journey through the vibrant streets of medieval Baghdad, Cordoba, and Cairo, where bustling libraries and grand mosques are learning hubs. You will meet luminaries like Ibn Sina, whose works in medicine guided physicians for centuries, and Ibn al-Haytham, whose pioneering approach to optics laid the groundwork for modern scientific methods. Inspiring Sir Issac Newton himself. You will see soon...

Al Jazari's crankshaft mechanism which became fundamental for Internal combustion engines driving our cars, trucks, ships, etc. You will also witness the architectural splendour of structures like the Alhambra and the Dome of the Rock, which stand as timeless testaments to the era's artistic ingenuity. Yet, this book is more than just a chronicle of past achievements. It reflects how the spirit of the Golden Age can inspire us today. As the world faces challenges that require collective ingenuity and cooperation, the lessons of this era remind us of the power of curiosity, openness, and a shared commitment to the betterment of humanity.

This book is written for a broad audience: those passionate about history, students and scholars seeking more profound insight, and anyone inspired by the idea that knowledge transcends borders and beliefs. It is an invitation to rediscover a period often overlooked in mainstream narratives but one that undeniably shaped the modern world.

I am deeply indebted to the countless scholars and translators who have preserved and illuminated the works of this era. Without their dedication, much of what we know about the Golden Age of Islam would remain hidden in manuscripts and forgotten archives.

I also acknowledge the richness of modern research and resources that have allowed us to continue exploring the achievements of this extraordinary time. As you turn these pages, I hope you will be as inspired as I have been by the visionaries of the Golden Age of Islam.

May their pursuit of knowledge and unwavering belief in the unity of science and faith ignite a spark in our quests for understanding and progress. Please share every chapter you read on social media and every sentence you find interesting, show them the need to read about our achievements, and encourage them to get the book themselves and potentially change their lives.

A point to note is that this book is not written by an accomplished scholar; on the contrary, I am just a student researching the Golden Age of Islam for over a year now, and this book is me sharing my knowledge in the crudest form possible. So, please be full of forgiveness if you find something that does not fit the bill.

Your suggestions are welcome, as this is not the end; this is just the beginning of a never-ending journey, as I have only "just scratched" the surface of this era in my research. I am only an email away. Please write to me: qalamaurkagaz@gmail.com.

Salim Khan-Founder- Qalam Aur Kagaz. November 24th, 2024.

PREPARING YOU FOR THE BOOK

Before you dive into the book, I would like to set a few points straight. First, the language used in the book is appreciative, critical, and straight to the point, but it sometimes exhibits my frustration. This is the need of the hour, and I have expressed myself openly.

Second, you will also see a few sentences being repeated at several places, e.g., *"This had a profound impact on Europe and the World"* I have not refrained from using this and other such sentences repeatedly because, to me, it is not redundancy, on the contrary, it shows the magnitude of what and how much we contributed (the fact that it is repeated several places only emphasis the number of ways and the number of times we contributed). I hope I made sense when I said that.

Here is a fun exercise for you: keep a pen and a piece of paper handy and note down how many times such sentences have been repeated; and then equate it directly to the amount of value we have added to the world that does not seem to acknowledge it with gratitude (At least with due credits).

Finally, I request you to treat this book as an academic work and not a religious work; what I mean by that is, I have not written this book as a Shia or a Sunni; I have written this book as a researcher who is profoundly affected by the subject of the book, and I have not taken any religious stand here while discussing specific sensitive topics (You will know when you read).

I am undeniably a Muslim, and I wish to present our achievements unequivocally.

INTRODUCTION TO THE GOLDEN AGE OF ISLAM WHAT IT WAS AND WHY IT MATTERS

The Golden Age of Islam lasted from the 8th to the 13th century and was a period of unparalleled intellectual and cultural flourishing in the Islamic world—the likes of which we haven't seen since. During this time, cities like Baghdad, Cordoba, Cairo, and Rey (in Iraq) rose as global knowledge and innovation hubs. Scholars from diverse backgrounds—Muslims, Christians, Jews, and Zoroastrians—collaborated to translate, preserve, and expand upon the knowledge of ancient civilisations.

This era matters profoundly because it laid the groundwork for many of the advancements, we take for granted today. This period's visionaries redefined fields like algebra, optics, and medicine and **defined** *the scientific method* used to date to prove any point. Beyond the sciences, the Golden Age also saw incredible achievements in literature, art, architecture, and philosophy, demonstrating the Islamic world's holistic approach to knowledge.

The Golden Age was not just about accumulating knowledge but about sharing and synthesising it. Through the translation movements, the establishment of academies like the Bayt al-Hikmah (House of Wisdom), and the dedication of scholars, the Islamic world became a bridge between the ancient and modern worlds, transmitting ideas to Europe and catalysing the Renaissance.

Understanding this era is crucial because it challenges modern narratives that often overlook or marginalise non-Western contributions to global progress. The Golden Age of Islam is a reminder of humanity's capacity for innovation when united by shared values of learning, curiosity, and respect for diversity.

The primary purpose of this book is to celebrate and illuminate the achievements of the Golden Age of Islam. It aims to:

- Educate readers about the profound contributions of Muslim scholars to various fields, from medicine and mathematics to literature and architecture.
- Bridge historical gaps, highlighting how the knowledge preserved and advanced during this era influenced subsequent developments in Europe and beyond.
- Inspire a renewed appreciation for the values of curiosity, collaboration, and intellectual rigour that defined the era.
- Counter stereotypes, offering a balanced and nuanced understanding of Islam's rich intellectual heritage and its emphasis on the pursuit of knowledge.

Yes, Muslims contributed to the world just as much as other civilisations. I would argue we did a lot more than any other civilisation, and no, Muslims are not just Terrorists!

The book also seeks to connect the past with the present, demonstrating how the spirit of the Golden Age can guide us in addressing modern challenges. By showcasing the era's achievements and the principles underpinning them, it encourages readers to embrace diversity, foster dialogue, and contribute to a more interconnected world. Most importantly, reviewing this era ensures that the next generation remembers their ancestral achievements, forms a deep connection, and takes inspiration to match them.

Above all, I acknowledge the wisdom of the Quran and the teachings of Prophet Muhammad (PBUH), which have continually emphasised the importance of seeking knowledge and understanding.

I offer my heartfelt thanks to all who contributed, knowingly or unknowingly. This book is a testament to the enduring legacy of the Golden Age of Islam and a humble attempt to share its light with the world.

A special thanks to my Social Media trolls who pushed me to research this topic by constantly abusing Muslims and Islam overall. This research and this book are utterly made possible because of the motivation that you provided, and thanks to you, potentially millions of Muslims will now be made aware of who we are and **Why it all Matters. Today!**

HISTORY

1

HISTORY IS ESSENTIAL. WITHOUT IT WE WOULD EXIST IN A VACUUM

"History is the root of wisdom and the storehouse of experience. It enlightens our understanding of the world and guides us toward a better future by teaching us the lessons of those who came before."

– Ibn Khaldun

Rise of Islam

The Golden Age of Islam began after Islam's rise in the 7th century CE, a transformative era initiated by the Prophet Muhammad (PBUH) (We cannot ignore the foundation Islam laid for the Golden Age of Islam to flourish). Born in Mecca in 570 CE, Prophet Muhammad received divine revelations at 40, which would form the Quran, Islam's holy book. His teachings emphasised monotheism, justice, compassion, and the pursuit of knowledge as worship.

The early Islamic community, the Ummah, was built on principles of equality, social justice, and accountability. By the time Prophet Muhammad passed away in 632 CE, Islam had united the Arabian Peninsula under a single faith and established the foundations of governance that would shape its future civilisations.

The Rashidun Caliphate (632–661 CE) succeeded the Prophet, characterised by the leadership of the Caliphs. During this period:

*   Abu Bakr (RA), the first caliph, consolidated the Arabian Peninsula under Islamic rule.
*   Umar ibn al-Khattab (RA) oversaw the expansion of Islam into the Byzantine and Sassanid empires, laying the groundwork for a global civilisation.
*   Uthman ibn Affan (RA) compiled the Quran into a single, standardised text.
*   Ali ibn Abi Talib (RA) emphasised principles of justice and equity amidst political challenges.
*   This era saw the beginnings of Islamic governance, which emphasised consultation (shura), welfare (zakat), and justice and facilitated ethical administration and scholarship.

The Abbasid Caliphate (750–1258 CE) represents the zenith of the Islamic Golden Age. After overthrowing the Umayyad Caliphate, the Abbasids established their capital in Baghdad in 762 CE under Caliph Al-Mansur. Strategically located along the Tigris River, Baghdad became a focus point of cultures, ideas, and trade.

The Abbasid era shifted focus from military conquests to intellectual and cultural pursuits. Key highlights include:

The establishment of a merit-based administration that welcomed contributions from Persians, Arabs, and other ethnicities. This was critical in the progress that was made. Encouragement of translations of Greek, Persian, and Indian works into Arabic, preserving classical knowledge while stimulating new ideas. Without this, Greek knowledge would have withered away, as by the time of the Renaissance, most critical manuscripts from the Greeks were transmitted in Arabic. This by no means is indicative that Greek work didn't survive; it only meant extensive work was available in Arabic.

There is an emphasis on urban development, which transformed cities like Baghdad, Basra, and Samarkand into thriving centres of learning and trade. First-ever Hospitals were established in Baghdad. It's a fascinating story of how Al Razi decided on which spot to choose for the hospitals (don't miss that story).

This knowledge synthesis exemplified Islam's embrace of diverse intellectual traditions, laying the foundation for innovations in medicine, astronomy, mathematics, and more.

Note: It would be childish to say the Golden Age of Islam was a mere translation movement. Muslims didn't contribute to the world except by translating original manuscripts into another language only to be made available to the Europeans. However, we must acknowledge that translation played a significant part in forming the base upon which several *corrections* were made, refined and then presented as a treatise (A "treatise" is a formally and systematically written work) by giants of the Golden Age of Islam, including several discoveries and inventions that have stood the test of time and are relevant even today. Another point of contention is it was not just Muslims who set the gold standards in innovation; there were Christians, Zoroastrians, and Jews, so why call it the Golden Age of "Islam"? At the outset, let me address this point and set the foundations for this jaw-dropping (I kid you not!) journey of being shocked (post-reading the book).

Dr APJ Abdul Kalam Azad was the most prolific scientist India has ever produced; there is no controversy about that; he is rightly called "The Missile Man" of India, and his contributions to India's Nuclear strength are known to all, so when we address our missiles, we say, "India's Nuclear Missile", do we say Dr APJ Abdul Kalam Azad's Nuclear Missile? It is so because India was the patron, and Dr Kalam worked for the Indian Government. Similarly, every scientist working in the House of Wisdom was funded by the Islamic Caliph; hence, all credit goes to the Islamic Caliphate.

2

THE GREAT BAYT HIKMAH OR
THE HOUSE OF WISDOM

"Islamic civilization was one of the most marvelous that ever flourished, and in the medieval world, the Arabs were the unparalleled masters of science."

– Gustave Le Bon (while referring to Bayt Al Hikmah)

The House of Wisdom.

This book addresses the most critical pillar of the Golden Age of Islam, The House of Wisdom (Bayt al-Hikmah). Established in Baghdad during the 8th century CE under the Abbasid Caliphate, it became a cornerstone of the Islamic Golden Age, embodying a profound commitment to intellectual pursuit and cross-cultural collaboration. Initially founded as a library under Caliph Harun al-Rashid, it reached its zenith under Caliph Al-Ma'mun, who transformed it into a comprehensive learning academy. The House of Wisdom was a hub for the translation movement, where scholars like Hunayn ibn Ishaq, a Christian polymath, translated Greek, Persian, and Indian texts into Arabic. This effort preserved and synthesised the intellectual heritage of ancient civilisations.

Beyond Baghdad, major libraries were established in cities like Cordoba, Cairo, and Damascus. The library of Cordoba, under Caliph Al-Hakam II, reportedly housed over 400,000 manuscripts, making it one of the largest libraries of its time.

Madrasas (educational institutions) and private libraries flourished, ensuring that knowledge reached scholars and students in remote areas. Institutions like the observatories at Maragha and Samarkand combined practical experimentation with theoretical studies, contributing to fields like astronomy and engineering. These academies became places where scholars debated, innovated, and collaborated, setting the stage for modern scientific methodologies.

Beyond translation, scholars like Al-Khwarizmi, the father of algebra, and Al-Kindi, a philosopher and mathematician, made groundbreaking contributions in mathematics, astronomy, medicine, Ibn al Haytham set ground rules for scientific demonstration and single handedly defined the field of Optics that became the benchmark for future scientists like Issac Newton.

Thabit ibn Qurra advanced geometry and mechanics, expanding on works by Archimedes and Euclid, while astronomers and mathematicians refined trigonometry and astronomical tables. These advancements influenced Islamic science and European Renaissance figures like

Copernicus. The impact of the House of Wisdom extended to practical applications such as navigation, engineering, and medicine. Its inclusive and multilingual approach facilitated the preservation and dissemination of critical knowledge, ensuring the survival of ancient texts and fostering original discoveries. Under Al-Ma'mun's patronage, rare manuscripts were acquired from Byzantium, India, and other regions, creating one of history's most comprehensive collections of intellectual resources. This systematic effort, funded by the Abbasid state, sought to preserve and expand ancient knowledge. The translation process was meticulously organised, involving scholars from diverse religious and cultural backgrounds.

Manuscripts from Greek, Indian, and Persian traditions—such as those by Aristotle, Ptolemy, Hippocrates, and Brahmagupta—were brought to Baghdad, often through diplomatic missions or military campaigns. By military campaign, I mean when Muslims won, instead of asking for Gold as compensation, they would ask for all of their books. Al Mamun is said to have told his court attendees that he wanted all the knowledge the world has to exist within the boundaries of Baghdad. Texts were first translated into Syriac if they were Greek, then into Arabic, ensuring accuracy and accessibility. Hunayn ibn Ishaq then refined these works by adding commentaries and contextual explanations to clarify complex ideas. Scholars also developed specialised glossaries to standardise technical terms across translations.

Acquiring these manuscripts required extensive geographic outreach. The Abbasid caliphs negotiated with rulers from distant lands, including the Byzantine Empire and India, to secure rare texts. For example, Al-Ma'mun maintained diplomatic relations with Emperor Theophilos of Byzantium, acquiring manuscripts such as Ptolemy's Almagest and other Greek classics, often as part of peace negotiations or in exchange for financial incentives. Manuscripts from India, like Brahmagupta's Brahmasphutasiddhanta, introduced advanced mathematics and astronomy, while Persian sources provided invaluable knowledge in medicine, administration, and literature. Yet, while they gathered all the information the manuscripts contained, the scholars didn't hold back in criticising the earlier giants and often correcting them. E.g. the famous book written by Ibn al Haytham is known as "Shukuk Ala Batlaymus", meaning "Doubts Concerning Ptolemy". Can you imagine going against Ptolemy, whose work was considered a benchmark? An analogy would be to go against Albert Einstein, challenging his theory of relativity!

However, the Abbasid caliphs played a crucial role in fostering this intellectual environment and encouraged criticism and out-of-the-box thinking. Al-Ma'mun, in particular, was deeply invested in knowledge, allocated substantial state funding and offered high salaries to translators and scholars. He participated in theological and scientific debates.

The translation movement produced profound results, preserving the intellectual heritage of ancient civilisations while fostering original contributions. Scholars at the House of Wisdom, such as Al-Khwarizmi, developed new mathematical theories like algebra (From his book Al Jabr wa Al Muqabala) and algorithms (the word is derived from his name Al Khawarizmi to Algorithmi), introduced the Hindu-Arabic numeral system, and refined the concept of zero—revolutionising calculations and laying the foundation for modern mathematics. Al-Kindi merged Greek philosophy with Islamic thought, advancing logic, cryptography, and music theory. While cryptography existed earlier, his use became the most refined and is still considered one of the best forms of Cryptography.

I have discussed this in detail with an example in the coming chapters. The House of Wisdom's legacy extends far beyond the Islamic world. Many translated works, along with their commentaries and expansions, were later translated into Latin and became the cornerstone of the European Renaissance. Figures like Fibonacci, Copernicus, and Descartes relied on these texts, transforming ancient ideas into tools for future innovation. I am sure you are curious by now about the "Structure" called "Bayt Al-Hikmah", so let me address that now. Some records state that we have no known information about the physical vastness of Bayt Al-Hikmah, where it was located, whether it was a symbolic name, or whether it existed.

Other records mention a place within the Abbasid Palace, which had extensive libraries where manuscripts were stored, where scholars had free access and would often meet to discuss their findings and learnings.

There has to be a place that existed. Where else would you store such massive manuscripts and findings? We can debate whether it was a separate building or within the palace; it is a valid point of discussion. And if there was a place, why were there no traces of it left behind? I blame the Mongols for that. It is a universal knowledge that Mongols destroyed every place they invaded to the last bit. Irrespective of the presence or the absence of a physical structure, what is not contentious is the fact that it played a significant role in bringing people from far-off lands to collaborate on some of the monumental projects initiated there within and further the knowledge to make the world wiser and intellectually more advance.

3

THE GREATEST POLYMATH...MAYBE!

"The soul is like a mirror that reflects the divine truth, but it can only reflect clearly when it is free from the distractions of the material world."

– Ibn Sina

(Note: You will know why I say "maybe" in 9th chapter)

Abu Ali al-Husayn ibn Abdullah ibn Sina or Ibn Sina (Avicenna) and His *"Canon of Medicine"*

Ibn Sina, also known as Avicenna (980–1037 CE), is one of the most celebrated physicians and philosophers of the Islamic Golden Age. His monumental work, *Al-Qanun fi al-Tibb* (The Canon of Medicine), became a cornerstone of medical knowledge for centuries.

A five-volume encyclopaedia that systematised medical knowledge from Greek, Indian, and earlier Islamic sources. Topics covered included anatomy and physiology, diagnosis and treatment of diseases, pharmacology and the properties of drugs. The *Canon* was the *first* to introduce innovative concepts such as the contagious nature of diseases like ***tuberculosis*** and the spread of infection through water and soil (read it again and let that sink in). Translated into Latin in the 12th century, it became a standard medical textbook in European universities until the 17th century. Ibn Sina's clinical observation and systematic experimentation laid the groundwork for modern medical practices and emphasised physical and psychological health integration.

He advocated for preventative care, balanced diets, and lifestyle adjustments as part of treatment. (Dieticians, I hope you are reading this!) These ideas were adopted in their entirety in European Universities. Ibn Sina's *Canon of Medicine* had an extraordinary impact on the development of medical education and practice in Europe. Below is a detailed exploration of how his ideas were embraced and advanced in major European institutions: the Translation Movement and Ibn Sina's Entry into Europe.

Ibn Sina's *Canon of Medicine* was translated into Latin in the 12th century by Gerard of Cremona, a prominent translator in Toledo, Spain.

a. The translation was part of the broader Toledo School of Translators movement, where Arabic texts were rendered Into Latin, bridging the gap between the Islamic world and medieval Europe. Ever wonder why when Muslims translated Greek into Arabic and then made enormous discoveries and yet are deliberately deemed "just translators", and yet when Europe did the same, they were deemed "innovators"? (Double Standards...Eh?).

b. The *Canon* quickly spread across European medical schools, forming the backbone of medical curricula from the 13th to the 17th century. Alongside Galen and Hippocrates, Ibn Sina became a central figure in European medical thought, often called the "Prince of Physicians." I have listed a few major universities where his book had thousands of disciples. (p.s: he lived like a prince too).

University of Salerno (Italy):
The *Canon* was a foundational text at the University of Salerno, among the earliest European medical schools. Ibn Sina's emphasis on clinical observation and systematic diagnosis influenced the school's focus on practical medicine.

University of Montpellier (France):
The *Canon* was required reading for medical students at Montpellier, which became a hub for Arabic-influenced medical education. Students at Montpellier were particularly drawn to Ibn Sina's integration of pharmacology and therapeutic techniques.

University of Bologna (Italy):
Known as one of the oldest universities in Europe, Bologna adopted the *Canon* for its systematic approach to teaching medical theory and practice. The text's classification of diseases and remedies was studied extensively, influencing the university's curriculum structure.

University of Paris (France):
The Faculty of Medicine in Paris treated Ibn Sina's *Canon* as a core medical authority, alongside works by Galen.
    His ideas on diagnostics, such as pulse and urine analysis, were emphasised in practical training.

Oxford and Cambridge Universities:
To many, this would be the highest form of denial. However, this is the reality. Ibn Sina's *Canon* was studied extensively and was a part of their formal curriculum for centuries. Al Razi was another whose work was

extensively studied. Al Razi was the one who set up the first hospitals in the world. The most outstanding physician of the medieval world. You will see it soon. The impact of his work was such that The *Canon* continued to show its relevance until the 17th century. One will find it hard to name another book with such a magnitude. I urge you to jog your mind and try to come up with another name.

It would be a disservice to Ibn Sina not to discuss some of his significant contributions to medicine and how they shaped modern medicine. I have broken this down into distinctive points for ease of understanding. Even so, I would not be able to list many of his incredible contributions within the scope of this book. If I were to summarise them, he and his work would demand another 400-page book in itself. Nevertheless, here is the list.

Medical Diagnostics:
European physicians adopted his detailed *pulse and urine analysis* methods as essential diagnostic tools. His categorisation of diseases and symptoms allowed for more precise diagnosis, replacing less systematic approaches. While researching and writing, I often zoned out relating to how physicians diagnose the disease; how frequently do you notice they ask for blood and urine samples? This was the brainchild of Ibn Sina.

Public Health and Contagion:
Ibn Sina's emphasis on quarantine and the spread of diseases through air and water inspired public health measures during epidemics in Europe, including the Black Death in the 14th century—oh, the Black Death and its impact. Often referred to as the Bubonic Plague, it killed nearly half of the European population. Of the different methods of medication put forth by Galen and Hippocrates proved ineffective, the only solution was "quarantine", something Ibn Sina had already emphasised hundreds of years prior in case of contagious diseases. During the Black Death (1347–1351 CE), European public health officials turned to Ibn Sina's writings for guidance on containment strategies:

His concepts of quarantine, derived from his understanding of contagion, were implemented in many cities. Ibn Sina's emphasis on clean air and sanitation was directly responsible for controlling the spread of the plague. Though imperfectly applied, these measures reflected a growing reliance on scientific principles over superstition, a shift mainly attributable to the influence of the *Canon of Medicine*. Europeans learned the hard lesson that medicine is superior to superstition, which was the direct impact of Ibn Sina.

Pharmacology:
Ibn Sina's cataloguing of medicinal substances influenced the development of European pharmacopoeias. His methods of testing drug efficacy and dosages were integrated into apothecaries' practices. This, coupled with the strategies suggested by Al Razi, including a new concept of in-house pharmacy in hospitals (more on this later), was crucial for ease of medication and availability.

Mental Health:
His writings on the connection between mental and physical health shaped early European approaches to psychiatry. Concepts such as treating melancholia (depression) and anxiety with environmental changes and therapy were revolutionary for the time. Two civilisations, one where mental issue was directly deemed to be demonic possession and the other where it was treated with therapy and specialised treatment.

Surgery and Anatomy:
While Ibn Sina did not perform dissections, his detailed descriptions of anatomy based on earlier Greek works informed European anatomical studies.

Surgeons like Guy de Chauliac incorporated Ibn Sina's surgical guidelines into their manuals. It is only evident that Ibn Sina profoundly impacted the physicians and surgeons in Europe. Should we list a few who integrated his methods?

Constantine the African:
A scholar at the Salerno School, Constantine translated many Arabic medical texts and introduced Ibn Sina's ideas to Italy, solidifying the influence of the *Canon*.

William of Conches:

A 12th-century French philosopher who praised Ibn Sina for reconciling medicine with natural philosophy and ethics.

Roger Bacon:

An English scholar who admired Ibn Sina's systematic approach to observation and experimentation, seeing it as foundational to the scientific method.

Andreas Vesalius:

Although Vesalius later challenged some of Ibn Sina's anatomical descriptions, his work was built upon the foundation of knowledge transmitted through the *Canon*.

By the 13th century, European universities had adopted the *Canon of Medicine* as a *required* text. Its use persisted until the Renaissance, demonstrating its unparalleled authority in medical education. Ibn Sina's detailed classifications of diseases, treatments, and drug properties standardised a previously fragmented field.

His approach encouraged consistency in medical diagnoses and treatments across Europe. The *Canon* served as a bridge between ancient medical knowledge and Renaissance advancements. Ibn Sina introduced systematic, evidence-based methodologies that indirectly influenced figures like Paracelsus and Ambroise Paré.

Even after the *Canon* fell out of favour in medical schools during the 17th century, its impact lingered:

The emphasis on observation, experimentation, and evidence-based treatment became a cornerstone of modern medicine. Ibn Sina's integration of physical, mental, and spiritual health continues to inspire holistic approaches in contemporary healthcare. The translation and dissemination of the *Canon* exemplify how cross-cultural collaboration can drive progress, a lesson that remains relevant in today's globalised world.

Ibn Sina was a polymath and a multifaceted personality who contributed to more than medicine. This book won't do justice to him if it doesn't highlight his other significant achievements, which go unnoticed overall. In the following subchapter, I list only a few of this incredible man's career achievements.

Ibn Sina was not only a physician but also a philosopher, scientist, and polymath whose influence extended well beyond medicine. His works in metaphysics, logic, astronomy, and natural sciences profoundly shaped intellectual traditions in both the Islamic world and Europe. Below is a detailed exploration of his contributions outside medicine and their lasting influence.

Ibn Sina is regarded as one of the greatest philosophers of the Islamic Golden Age, often referred to as the "Aristotle of Islam." His works bridged Greek philosophy with Islamic thought and heavily influenced medieval European philosophy. *Kitab al-Shifa* (The Book of Healing) includes a section on metaphysics where Ibn Sina explores the nature of existence.

The distinction between *essence* (what a thing is) and *existence* (that a thing is) emphasises that existence must be granted by a necessary being (God).

His metaphysical ideas were central to the works of European philosophers like Thomas Aquinas, who integrated Ibn Sina's thoughts into Christian theology.

The Floating Man Thought Experiment:
Ibn Sina introduced the "floating man" thought experiment to demonstrate human self-awareness and the soul's immaterial nature. This idea influenced later philosophical discussions on consciousness and self-awareness in the Islamic world and Europe.

Ibn Sina made significant astronomical advancements, focusing on celestial mechanics and observational methods. In *Kitab al-Najat* (The Book of Salvation), Ibn Sina described the motion of planets and the composition of heavenly spheres.

He rejected the Aristotelian notion of celestial bodies being composed of an unchanging "fifth element," proposing that they are subject to physical laws like those governing Earth.

While not fully heliocentric, Ibn Sina speculated on the dynamics of planetary motion, paving the way for Copernicus's later advancements. (AT Tusi, a polymath who worked at Maragha Observatory, played a significant role in influencing Copernicus and his heliocentric model. In a chapter dedicated to Astronomy, I write extensively about his *Couple,* which was later known as *Tusi Couple.* (This is one of the biggest revelations in the book).

European astronomers seeking to understand the universe beyond the Ptolemaic model referred to his works. Ibn Sina improved instruments like the astrolabe for more precise astronomical observations. These tools influenced European astronomers during the Renaissance, aiding navigation and star mapping.

Ibn Sina expanded Aristotelian logic and developed original epistemological theories (the study of knowledge). Ibn Sina refined the concept of modal logic (dealing with necessity and possibility), going beyond Aristotle by systematising the relationships between propositions.

Medieval logicians, including William of Ockham, studied his logical frameworks, which contributed to advancements in deductive reasoning.

Ibn Sina described how humans acquire knowledge through:

Perception: Gained through senses,
Reasoning: Through the intellect's ability to abstract universal truths from experiences.

His epistemological framework influenced European debates on empiricism versus rationalism. Ibn Sina's contributions to physics, chemistry, and geology demonstrate his wide-ranging scientific curiosity.

Ibn Sina described concepts such as inertia and momentum before Newton's first law of motion. In his *Physics* section of *Kitab al-Shifa*, he analysed the nature of light, heat, and motion. He was one of the first to say that light is made up of particles (remarkable!). His theories on dynamics influenced later European scholars, such as Jean Buridan, who developed the theory of impetus. Ibn Sina rejected the mystical aspects of alchemy and approached the subject with scientific rigour.

He classified substances into mineral, vegetable, and animal origins, emphasising their properties and transformations. His scepticism toward alchemical transmutation influenced later European chemists, contributing to the development of modern chemistry (Though he contributed significantly to chemistry, the real father of chemistry is Jabir Ibn Hayyan; I put forth my points in a separate chapter dedicated to him). Ibn Sina proposed theories about the origin of mountains, fossils, and earthquakes, attributing them to natural processes rather than supernatural causes. His geological observations inspired Renaissance scholars to explore Earth's processes scientifically.

Ibn Sina was also a poet and author, expressing complex philosophical ideas through artistic forms. *Hayy ibn Yaqzan* (Alive, Son of the Awake) is a symbolic story about self-discovery, divine knowledge, and the nature of reality.

His allegories inspired similar works in medieval Europe and influenced later thinkers such as Dante Alighieri. His works, especially *The Canon of Medicine* and *The Book of Healing*, became part of the European educational canon. Universities like Paris, Bologna, and Padua made his texts mandatory for medicine, philosophy, and natural sciences students. Thinkers like Michael Scot and Gerard of Cremona translated his works into Latin, ensuring their widespread dissemination. Commentaries by Albertus Magnus and Thomas Aquinas popularised his ideas among European intellectuals.

Ibn Sina's synthesis of Greek philosophy and Islamic thought helped reignite European interest in Aristotle, Plato, and scientific inquiry. His emphasis on logic, experimentation, and observation bridged the gap between medieval scholasticism and Renaissance humanism. Ibn Sina's contributions spanned multiple disciplines, demonstrating the interconnected nature of knowledge during the Islamic Golden Age. He achieved some of his best work before turning 30 years old. He is known to have begun the work on His *Canon* when he was merely 27 years of age. His ideas profoundly shaped European intellectual traditions, from medicine and astronomy to philosophy and natural sciences. By serving as a bridge between ancient wisdom and modern thought, Ibn Sina exemplifies the enduring legacy of the Islamic Golden

Age in global history. Remember not just the name Ibn Sina but also his legacy!

Just as Ibn Sina influenced medicine, Al Zahrawi influenced surgery. He revolutionised surgery by "opening people's brains" (pun intended) and showing how it was done!

4

HE SHOWED THEM HOW IT IS DONE!

"Medicine is an art as well as a science, and it requires the hand to be skilful and the heart to be compassionate."

– Al Zahrawi

Abu al-Qasim Khalaf ibn al-Abbas Al-Zahrawi, known as Albucasis in Latin (936–1013 CE), is regarded as the "Father of Modern Surgery." Living in Al-Andalus (modern-day Spain), he transformed surgical practices and medical education during the Islamic Golden Age. His monumental contributions to medicine, particularly surgery, laid the groundwork for centuries for surgical practices in the Islamic world and Europe. My approach to this chapter will be slightly different. I'd like to talk about how modern surgery was directly shaped by highlighting his methods and surgical equipment, as it is no joke to conceptualise and develop hundreds of them. The instruments that I refer to in the book are not works of an amateur, and proof of that is that most of his instruments are in use to this day! More than 1000 years later, he showed the world *how it is done*! And for that purpose, I have listed his achievements for the appropriate substantiation. This is a tiny list, yet quite humbling, as it shows the stature of what this man achieved in a single lifetime. In addition, I will talk about Ibn Zuhr who is another skilled surgeon, and we will discuss him later. For now, here are some of Al Zahrawi's achievements.

1. Authoring the Landmark Work: *Kitab al-Tasrif*
    Al-Zahrawi's *Kitab al-Tasrif li-man 'Ajiza 'an al-Ta'lif (The Method of Medicine)* is a 30-volume medical encyclopaedia that systematically covers various branches of medicine, including surgery, pharmacy, and therapeutics. He detailed the surgical techniques, instruments, and post-operative care. He Illustrated diagrams of over 200 surgical tools, many of which he invented or refined. The surgical volume of *Kitab al-Tasrif* was translated into Latin by Gerard of Cremona in the 12th century. It became a cornerstone of surgical education in European universities for over 500 years. In the modern world, where science keeps advancing, essentially overwriting most earlier works, his work was relevant for 500 years. If this is not substantial enough for the world to acknowledge him, what is?

2. Pioneering Techniques in Surgery
    Al-Zahrawi introduced innovative surgical techniques, many of which were revolutionary for his time.

a. Cauterisation: Advocated for cauterisation to stop bleeding and treat wounds, introducing methods to minimise pain and infection.

    Ligature of Arteries: Used ligatures to control bleeding, a practice later credited to Ambroise Paré in the 16th century.

b. Bone Fracture Treatment: Developed methods for setting bones and immobilising fractures using splints and bandages.

His techniques became standard practices in both the Islamic world and medieval Europe.

3. Establishing Plastic and Reconstructive Surgery

    Al-Zahrawi is considered one of the earliest pioneers in plastic and reconstructive surgery. He performed procedures to repair facial injuries, including rhinoplasty (reconstruction of the nose), and innovated methods to treat disfigurements caused by trauma or disease. His contributions were foundational to the development of modern plastic surgery.

4. Advancements in Obstetrics and Gynaecology

    Al-Zahrawi made significant strides in women's health, particularly obstetrics and gynaecology. He designed specialised tools, including forceps, to assist in childbirth. He also wrote extensively on caesarean sections, complications during labour, and post-natal care. His writings improved maternal and neonatal care in the Islamic world and influenced European gynaecological practices.

5. Introduction of Dental Surgery and Toothpaste.

    Al-Zahrawi is one of the earliest documented surgeons to describe dental care and oral surgery techniques. He described the extraction of diseased teeth, using gold threads to stabilise loose teeth, and developed methods for cleaning and whitening teeth. European dentists referenced his writings on dental surgery well into the Renaissance.

    He gave the world Toothpaste. He was the foremost person who used salt in toothpaste for its abrasive properties and clove due to its anti-bacterial properties. Mint was used to get rid of odour and help freshen breath. Charcoal from the bark of the tree was used in powdered form. Surprisingly, he used Honey and vinegar as well. He made toothpaste in three forms: Miswak, powder, and gargling water solution; who would have thought it?

6. Innovating Surgical Sutures
    Al-Zahrawi introduced catgut sutures, a significant advancement in wound care and healing.
    Why Catgut?
    Catgut (derived from animal intestines) is naturally absorbable, eliminating the need for suture removal. This innovation became a standard in surgery and is still used in modern medicine.

7. Contributions to Pharmacology
    In addition to his surgical expertise, Al-Zahrawi was a skilled pharmacist who explored the preparation and application of medicines. He documented methods for compounding medications, including syrups, ointments, and pills. Innovated tools for drug administration, such as syringes for delivering medicines directly to the body. His contributions influenced the development of pharmacy as a distinct discipline.

8. Early Concepts of Anesthesia
    Al-Zahrawi advocated for the use of sedation during surgical procedures to reduce pain and distress. He used herbal mixtures and inhalable anaesthetics derived from opium and mandrake. His early use of anaesthesia was a precursor to modern pain management in surgery.

9. Emphasis on Surgical Education and Ethics
    Al-Zahrawi was deeply committed to educating future generations of surgeons. His *Kitab al-Tasrif* was a comprehensive guide for surgical training, emphasising hands-on experience and the importance of anatomy. He stressed the importance of ethical practice, including

treating patients with dignity and prioritising their welfare. His teachings became a benchmark for surgical education in Europe and the Islamic world.

Let me highlight the equipment I initially boasted about; read carefully, and you will understand why they are worth the brag. Among the 200 pieces of surgical equipment he designed, I have listed below a few of the most important ones that revolutionised surgery deep into the Renaissance. In addition to developing surgical equipment, I have also mentioned how he used it to refine surgery through his groundbreaking surgical techniques.

1. Scalpels and Blades

    Al-Zahrawi described various types of scalpels for cutting soft tissue, each with unique shapes and sizes.

    These included straight and curved blades to accommodate different surgical needs. They are used for incisions during abscess drainage, tumour removal, and exploratory surgeries. His precise descriptions allowed future surgeons to replicate and adapt these instruments for various procedures.

2. Forceps

    Al-Zahrawi designed forceps for gripping and extracting objects like foreign bodies or stones. Specialised forceps for removing bone fragments, assisting in childbirth, and performing dental extractions. His forceps designs are still used in modern surgery with minimal modification.

3. Bone Saws and Drills

    He created saws and drills for orthopaedic procedures, focusing on safety and efficiency. They treat fractures, perform amputations, and remove bone deformities. These tools improved surgical outcomes and were widely adopted in later European medical practices. He advocated for splinting fractures and ensuring proper alignment before immobilisation. His detailed instructions improved outcomes in orthopaedic care.

4. Catheters and Dilator

    Al-Zahrawi introduced catheters and urethral dilators for urinary tract procedures. Some catheters were hollow to allow the passage of fluids or medicines. They relieve urinary retention and deliver treatments directly to the bladder. These tools advanced urology and inspired later developments in catheter technology. Al-Zahrawi described a minimally invasive method for removing bladder stones using specialised forceps and incisions. His method minimised pain and complications, advancing urological surgery in the Lithotomy (Bladder stone removal)

5. Surgical Needles and Sutures (sterile threads used to stitch wounds)

    He designed needles of various shapes and sizes for stitching wounds, including curved needles for internal sutures. He advocated for using absorbable catgut sutures made from animal intestines. They were used in wound closure, internal surgeries, and cosmetic repairs. Catgut sutures became a *standard* in surgery after his introduction and usage. He emphasised the importance of suturing internal and external wounds with precision. He used catgut sutures for internal wounds, which dissolved naturally. His suturing methods reduced healing time and complications. Also, it significantly reduced pain caused by the fact that the sutures were not required to be removed. If you ever needed to get stitches and wondered how they dissolved by themselves, you know now and also who put forth the idea first!

6. Cautery Tools

    Al-Zahrawi developed a range of cautery instruments for sealing wounds and stopping bleeding. These included heated metal rods of various shapes for different applications. They treat wounds, stop haemorrhages, and remove skin growths. He advocated for controlled cauterisation to stop bleeding, treat wounds, and remove tumours. He developed over 50 specialised cautery tools for different applications. He introduced a method for safely removing tonsils using a curved blade and cauterisation. These techniques reduced the risk of infection and, therefore, proved to be lifesaving.

7. Speculums

    Al-Zahrawi invented vaginal and rectal speculums with adjustable blades to facilitate examinations and procedures. They are used in gynaecology to diagnose and treat fistulas and uterine prolapse. Speculums-inspired modern designs are still used in gynaecological practices. He introduced tools like forceps to assist in difficult deliveries. Thus significantly reducing danger to the lives of both mother and baby.

8. Dental Instruments

    Created tools for tooth extraction, scaling, and cleaning. Pincers were introduced to stabilise loose teeth and devices for filling cavities. Al-Zahrawi's dental tools were among the first systematically designed for oral surgeries.

    Al-Zahrawi's contributions to surgical tools and techniques were transformative, bridging ancient practices with modern innovations. His meticulous documentation of tools and methods in *Kitab al-Tasrif* ensured the dissemination of his knowledge across cultures, profoundly influencing surgical practices in the Islamic world and Europe. In addition, the earliest known definition of "**Syringe**" was given by Al Zahrawi. This does not mean someone didn't talk about it before him; it means it was Al Zahrawi who defined the purpose of the Syringe, and such is followed to this day.

The impact of Al-Zahrawi during and after the Golden Age is irreversible and far-reaching. His innovations elevated surgery from a *lowly trade* to a *respected science* within Islamic medicine. It inspired later Islamic surgeons like Ibn Zuhr.

Kitab al-Tasrif was a required text in European universities, such as Salerno and Bologna, well into the 16th century. European surgeons like Guy de Chauliac and Ambroise Paré cited Al-Zahrawi extensively, incorporating his methods into their practices. Al-Zahrawi's surgical instruments and techniques influenced the development of modern surgery. His emphasis on patient care and surgical ethics remains foundational to medical practice. His work was taken up and furthered by many noted physicians; one such we will discuss is Abū-Marwān 'Abd al-Malik ibn Abī al-'Alā' Ibn Zuhr or as known in Latin Avenzoar.

Ibn Zuhr, one of the most distinguished physicians of the Islamic Golden Age, made transformative contributions to medicine, particularly in clinical observation, surgery, pharmacology, and medical ethics. Born in Al-Andalus (modern Spain) in 1091 CE, Ibn Zuhr emphasised hands-on clinical practice and meticulous patient examination, setting a *precedent* for modern diagnostic methods. While documenting their symptoms and treatments, he provided some of the earliest, most accurate descriptions of diseases, including pericarditis, throat infections, and skin disorders such as scabies. His work also demonstrated a groundbreaking approach to experimental medicine, as he tested surgical procedures and drug efficacy on animals before applying them to humans, establishing the foundation for modern experimental methodologies.

Ibn Zuhr's pioneering techniques in surgery included performing tracheotomies for airway obstructions and introducing advanced methods for abscess drainage and wound care, showcasing a mastery that *elevated* surgical practices. His contributions extended to pharmacology, where he developed personalised treatments tailored to individual patients and documented numerous herbal remedies. Ibn Zuhr also emphasised the critical role of diet and nutrition in health, prescribing therapeutic diets as part of his holistic approach to medicine. His seminal text, *Kitab al-Taysir fi al-Mudawat wa al-Tadbir* (*The Book of Simplification Concerning Therapeutics and Diet*), combined practical advice on therapeutics, surgery, and dietetics with groundbreaking insights, becoming a cornerstone of medical education in both the Islamic world and Europe. Translated into Latin by Gerard of Cremona, this work significantly influenced European medical schools such as Salerno, Bologna, and Montpellier.

A staunch advocate of medical ethics, Ibn Zuhr emphasised the physician's duty to prioritise patient welfare, practice honesty, and maintain humility. He collaborated with Ibn Rushd (Known as Averroes in Latin), intertwining empirical and philosophical knowledge and further enriching the intellectual tradition of Al-Andalus. Ibn Zuhr's experimental methods and ethical practice shaped the medical field in the Islamic world and resonated deeply in Europe, where his works were studied and cited for centuries. His integration of experimental science with clinical medicine bridged the Islamic and European traditions, leaving a legacy that exemplified the enduring spirit of the Golden Age of Islam.

I will list a few of his achievements, staying consistent with the theme of the chapter. However, I will take the liberty of being a writer and bring his most significant contribution to light. This innovation has saved countless lives and is followed ardently even today whenever a new drug is tested. Let us begin with this.

The concept of testing drugs on animals before rolling out for public use:

Yet again, I address the controversial topic of drug testing by saying Ibn Zuhr was the first person to introduce and extensively promote the idea of testing drugs on animals before they could be mass-produced. Thus, he saved countless lives during his lifetime, and for more than a thousand years later, as a practice still being followed today! However, as always, let me bring the cat out of the box by discussing whether this happened before him and why he should get the credit.

It is a fact that before The Golden Age of Islam, there were a couple of advanced civilisations where this could have happened, including the Greek civilisation. Arguably, the most prominent physician among the Greeks was Galen. He used animals (primarily monkeys and pigs) to study anatomy and physiology. However, his focus was mainly on understanding the body rather than testing drugs or procedures for therapeutic purposes.

Ancient Indian medical texts like the Ayurveda and Sushruta Samhita referenced the observation of animals for medical insights, but they lacked the methodical approach Ibn Zuhr adopted for drug testing. Even Islamic physicians before him had a limited approach. Earlier Islamic physicians

28

such as Al-Razi and Ibn Sina advocated empirical observation and medical experimentation. However, their focus was more on clinical medicine and observations in human cases rather than explicitly recommending animal testing.

However, Ibn Zuhr went beyond the traditional approach by advocating the direct and systematic testing of drugs on animals to understand their effects. He conducted systematic surgeries and experimented thoroughly before applying them to humans, documenting this in detail in his seminal work *Kitab al-Taysir fi al-Mudawat wa al-Tadbir* (*The Book of Simplification Concerning Therapeutics and Diet*).

Below are some of his outstanding achievements.

1. Pioneering Clinical Observation: Ibn Zuhr emphasised direct patient examination and detailed recording of symptoms, which advanced diagnostic accuracy. This method became a cornerstone of clinical practice in the Islamic world and influenced European approaches to patient care, particularly in universities such as Montpellier and Salerno.

2. Detailed Disease Descriptions: He provided groundbreaking descriptions of diseases, such as pericarditis, throat infections, and skin conditions like scabies, distinguishing them from other ailments. His clarity in identifying specific symptoms greatly enhanced diagnostic precision and influenced European medical texts.

3. Surgical Innovations: He performed advanced surgical procedures, such as tracheotomies for airway obstructions and abscess drainage, and used antiseptic techniques to reduce infections. European surgeons later adopted and refined these practices, contributing to the evolution of surgery.

4. Pharmacological Advancements: Ibn Zuhr developed personalised medicinal treatments and documented numerous effective remedies using herbs and natural compounds. His work influenced

pharmacological practices in the Islamic world and provided a basis for European apothecaries and early pharmacology texts.

5. Holistic Approach to Medicine: He emphasised the role of diet and nutrition in health and prescribed specific dietary modifications for different illnesses. This integration of preventive care with therapeutic methods resonated in Islamic and European medical traditions, inspiring holistic approaches to health.

6. Seminal Medical Text: *Kitab al-Taysir*: His book, *Kitab al-Taysir fi al-Mudawat wa al-Tadbir* (*The Book of Simplification Concerning Therapeutics and Diet*), combined practical medical advice with theoretical insights. It became a crucial reference in the Islamic world and Renaissance Europe. Gerard of Cremona's Latin translation ensured its wide dissemination.

7. Ethical Medical Practice: Ibn Zuhr stressed physicians' ethical responsibilities, advocating honesty, patient welfare, and humility in medical practice. His principles influenced Islamic medical ethics and later shaped European medical oaths and codes of conduct.

8. Collaboration with Ibn Rushd (Averroes): Working with the philosopher Ibn Rushd, Ibn Zuhr integrated empirical and philosophical approaches to medicine, enriching the intellectual legacy of Al-Andalus. Their collaboration influenced European scholasticism and medical thought.

9. Transmission of Knowledge to Europe: Ibn Zuhr's works were translated into Latin and widely studied in European universities, such as Bologna and Montpellier. His practical approach to medicine bridged Islamic and European traditions, directly influencing the medical practices of the Renaissance.

These achievements cemented Ibn Zuhr's place as one of the most influential physicians of the Golden Age of Islam. Undoubtedly, Ibn Zuhr was noteworthy, but the most prominent physician of the medieval world, not just Islamic, is by far and uncontroversially Al Razi. He played an instrumental role in setting up the first Hospitals in the world in the 9th century. First hospitals in the 9th century? Were there no hospitals before that? The oldest record of civilisation goes back to Sumerians, almost 7000 years ago, so how could I dare say the first hospitals are only 1100 years old? The answer lies ahead in the next chapter.

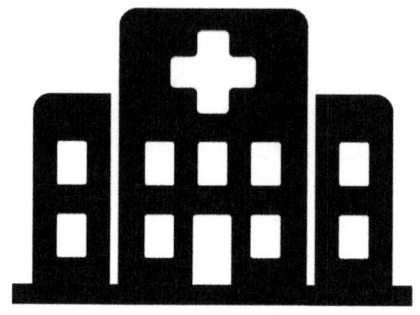

5

NO, THEY WERE NOT HOSPITALS

"Doubt is the key to knowledge, and questioning is the path to truth."

– Al Razi

I have habitually started the chapters with more on a substantial and controversial note. However, I have also made my points within the first paragraph, addressing those points with appropriate backing. If I say the first hospitals were set up in Baghdad in the 9th century, were there no hospitals before the 9th century? At the outset, this sounds ridiculous and frankly incredulous. But wait. Let me put forth my points.

We are talking about the 9th century when Europe was thrown into the dark ages, religious dogmatic practises were widespread and European men were on a witch-hunt. A woman with any mental issues was considered a witch and a man possessed. At the same time, Al Razi was setting up a separate department for "patients" with mental disorders. That is perspective, right there!

Now, addressing the point, yes, there were physicians before the 9th century, and yes, people were treated, but not at any specific facility dedicated to treating patients in mass numbers. There were makeshift camps; patients visited the physicians, and vice versa. There has yet to be a single record of patients reeling under different types of illness being treated under one central roof. One does say that Indians were already performing plastic surgeries hundreds of years prior; at best, it happened in isolation and didn't develop into a structured practice.

However, Al Razi's hospitals were fully developed and functional following set patient treatment guidelines. For the first time in recorded history, an entrance exam was conducted to pick physicians treating patients. These physicians were fully trained and taught patient-doctor mannerisms, such as confidentiality and treating all patients equally, regardless of race, caste, religion, or financial status. Abbasid Caliphate set up patronage for the hospitals, ensuring treatment was done for free for those who could not afford it. Some departments include Surgery, Emergency, General Ward, Psychiatric, Maternity Ward, etc.

They had dedicated operation theatres where all kinds of surgeries were carried out. Al Razi ensured that these hospitals are not just that but also educational institutes and research centres training future generations of physicians, much like what we see today.

Abu Bakr Muhammad ibn Zakariya al-Razi, known in the West as Rhazes, was another towering figure of the Islamic Golden Age. Born in the city of Ray, near modern-day Tehran in Iran, in 865 CE, Al-Razi was raised in a thriving cultural and intellectual environment. Ray was a prominent centre for learning in the Islamic world, and Al-Razi's insatiable curiosity and prodigious intellect quickly distinguished him from his peers. Initially drawn to music and alchemy in his early years, he later turned to medicine, cementing his legacy as one of history's most outstanding physicians and medical innovators.

Al-Razi insisted that medical students and practitioners continually update their knowledge by studying the latest medical texts and engaging in discussions. His approach to medical education was highly progressive, emphasising the importance of *questioning* established expertise and relying on empirical evidence. This scientific rigour was exemplified in his works, which often challenged the prevailing medical theories of his time, including those of the revered Greek physician Galen.

For instance, Al-Razi disputed Galen's humoral theory by conducting experiments demonstrating inconsistencies in its principles. Al-Razi's hospitals also house well-equipped pharmacies that prepare and dispense medications (have you seen an in-house pharmacy in hospitals today. Guess where the practice started?). His hospitals also housed huge libraries for budding physicians **(Yet another first!).** He was a master chemist who developed innovative pharmaceutical techniques, including the distillation of alcohol for medicinal purposes and the preparation of compounds like mercurial ointments and mineral-based remedies. His approach to pharmacy was holistic, combining chemistry, botany, and medicine knowledge to create effective treatments.

Al-Razi's rise to prominence as a physician coincided with the flourishing of Baghdad, the capital of the Abbasid Caliphate, which was then a hub of learning and innovation. Recognising Al-Razi's extraordinary talent and deep understanding of medicine, Caliph Al-Muktafi appointed him as the chief physician of Baghdad's hospitals. Al-Razi's tenure in Baghdad saw him transform medical practice and healthcare delivery organisation, especially in hospital administration.

It is not just that he built hospitals; it is also noteworthy how he chose spots to make them. He would send people to different corners of cities and ask them to hang a fresh piece of meat and leave it there for a few days; the place where it rots the least is the place he would pick to build his hospitals. Oh, I almost forgot, he called his hospitals Bimaristan from the word Bimar (sick) stan (place).

Al-Razi's most remarkable achievements were his insistence on rationalism and scepticism in medicine. He encouraged physicians to think critically, avoid dogma, and base their practice on empirical evidence. This approach often put him at odds with his contemporaries, particularly those who adhered rigidly to the teachings of Galen or relied on superstition. He would take a massive dislike for those who would prefer to go to the street charlatans for treatment rather than visit an educated physician. Al-Razi's dedication to scientific inquiry extended beyond medicine to chemistry, philosophy, and theology. He was a polymath who believed that knowledge was interconnected and that understanding one field could enhance insights into another.

Al-Razi's contributions to medicine are monumental and foundational, establishing him as one of the most significant figures in medical history. His work revolutionised the field, moving it away from *superstition* and into the realm of *empirical science*. Al-Razi was a prolific scholar, writing over 200 works on medicine, chemistry, and philosophy, with several enduring as essential references for centuries. His most notable contributions include the comprehensive medical encyclopaedia *Kitab al-Hawi* (The Comprehensive Book on Medicine), translated into Latin as *Liber Continens* by Gerard of Cremona, which became a cornerstone of European medical education. Another seminal work was *Kitab al-Mansuri* (The Book of Medicine Dedicated to Al-Mansur), a concise manual for practical medicine. His groundbreaking treatise on smallpox and measles, *Kitab fi al-Jadari wa al-Hasba*, was *the first scientific differentiation* of these two diseases and remains a foundational text in dermatology and epidemiology. Few came after him, and fewer still who came before him who contributed to the field of medicine to such an extent that they influenced the entire continent and followed rigorously throughout hospitals for centuries later. Al Razi will go down in history as the man who took over the field of medicine during the age of witchcraft and witch-hunt and saved the lives of thousands, especially those with mental illness, for if it were not for him, they would be put to stake.

"The doctor aims to do good, even to our enemies; how much more to our friends. My profession forbids me to harm my kindred, as it is instituted for the benefit and welfare of the human race, and God imposed on physicians the oath not to compose mortiferous remedies."

He said and certainly lived by it. I will share with you a heartening note about Bimaristan of Baghdad. The Abbasid Caliphate didn't just set up these places to treat their citizens or travellers; they had set up separate dedicated Bimarstans for those injured during battle by the enemy's army. They were treated with equal respect, dignity, and care, while we see that in modern conflicts, doing that in the 9th century was, at least, a novelty! And the most considerate one to humankind.

Key Contributions:

1. Contributions to Clinical Medicine and Diagnostics
    He differentiated *smallpox* from *measles* based on detailed symptoms, such as rash patterns, fever progression, and patient responses. Recognising psychological factors in physical ailments helped him take a more holistic approach to diagnosis. European physicians adopted his case-based approach, influencing early diagnostic manuals and case reporting in medieval universities.

2. The Legacy of the *Kitab al-Hawi* (The Comprehensive Book on Medicine)
    The *Kitab al-Hawi* remains one of the most significant works in medical history due to its comprehensive coverage and original insights. The text's Latin translation, *Liber Continents*, was widely studied in medieval Europe.

They are a primary reference in medical schools such as Salerno, Montpellier, and Bologna. Its pharmacological sections influenced the formulation of early European pharmacopoeias.

3. Foundations of Epidemiology and Public Health
    Al-Razi's recognition of environmental and social factors in disease spread laid the foundation for epidemiology. Advocated for isolating patients with contagious diseases (following the path Ibn Sina took), a concept later used during the European plagues.

4. Al-Razi's Experimental Approach in Pharmacology
    Al-Razi approached pharmacology with scientific rigour, applying methods of experimentation to test the efficacy and safety of treatments. Categorised drugs by their effects on the body and introduced controlled dosing guidelines. He documented hundreds of natural and synthetic compounds, providing recipes for their preparation. Early European apothecaries and physicians adopted his pharmacological methods, leading to advancements in drug standardisation.

6. Al-Razi's Role as a Pioneer of Medical Ethics
    Al-Razi wrote extensively about physicians' ethical responsibilities, emphasising the importance of patient care and social justice in medicine. The physician must serve all patients, regardless of wealth or social status. Compassion and patience are central virtues for healthcare providers. His writings influenced later ethical treatises, such as those of Maimonides in the Jewish tradition and European adaptations of the Hippocratic Oath.

7. Surgical Advancements and Antiseptics
    While primarily a physician, Al-Razi contributed to surgery through his chemistry applications.
    *   Alcohol as an Antiseptic:
        Al-Razi was among the first to advocate for using distilled alcohol to clean wounds and surgical instruments, reducing infections.

- Surgical Techniques:
  Described procedures for abscess drainage, hernia repair, and bone setting.

Transmission to Europe:
European surgeons like Guy de Chauliac later adopted his surgical methods, who cited Al-Razi's works in his *Chirurgia Magna*.

8. Rejection of Superstition in Medicine
    Al-Razi actively criticised the reliance on superstition and unscientific practices in medical treatment. He advocated for rational, evidence-based approaches to treatment. Critiqued physicians who used amulets or charms, emphasising natural remedies instead. His rationalism influenced Europe's transition from mystical to empirical medicine during the Renaissance.

9. Philosophical Contributions to Medicine
    Al-Razi's philosophical background informed his medical theories, especially his views on the mind-body connection.
    - Integration of Philosophy and Medicine:
      Wrote about the influence of emotions on physical health, proposing therapies that combined physical treatments with counselling.
    Influence on Europe:
    - His holistic approach inspired European thinkers like Ibn Sina and, later, Renaissance humanists who sought to integrate philosophy with medical science.

10. Educational Reforms in Medicine
    Al-Razi was a dedicated teacher and mentor who emphasised the importance of continuous learning and practical training for physicians.
    - Innovative Teaching Methods:
    - Encouraged hands-on experience in hospitals, supplementing theoretical study with clinical practice.

- They are advocated for regular case discussions among medical students and practitioners.

Legacy:

- These practices became integral to medical education in Islamic and European institutions.

Transmission of Al-Razi's Legacy to Europe

1. Translation Movement
   - Gerard of Cremona's Latin translation of *Kitab al-Hawi* in the 12th century was a milestone in transmitting Al-Razi's ideas to Europe.
   - European scholars translated and widely referenced his other works, such as *The Book of Smallpox and Measles*.

2. Integration into European Medical Curricula
   - Universities in Salerno, Montpellier, and Bologna adopted Al-Razi's texts as foundational material.

   His systematic approach influenced European medical traditions, bridging ancient and modern practices.

3. Long-Term Impact
   - Al-Razi's ideas continued to shape public health, pharmacology, and hospital design in Europe well into the Renaissance.
   - His emphasis on observation, ethics, and experimentation set the stage for the scientific revolution.

Al-Razi's contributions to medicine, public health, and medical ethics were transformative. His innovative approach to diagnostics, pharmacology, and hospital organisation laid the groundwork for modern medical practices. Al-Razi bridged ancient knowledge with new scientific paradigms by rejecting superstition, prioritising empirical observation, and emphasising compassion, leaving an indelible mark on the Islamic Golden Age and European Renaissance.

Another giant of the Golden Age of Islam was the person who wrote commentaries on the mighty *Canon* by Ibn Sina. He is known as Ibn Nafis and was the first to prove **Galen** wrong. His discovery would have sent waves in medicine, as proving Galen wrong was no small feat. We shall see exactly how he did so and what his discovery was that shook the world!

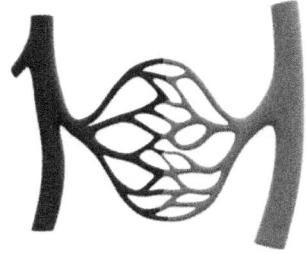

6

"GALEN YOU ARE WRONG", HE SAID

"Knowledge is not exclusive to a single nation or group; it is a universal gift meant to illuminate the minds and hearts of all humanity."

– Ibn Nafis

Honestly, I almost forgot to add him to the book. Hundreds of scholars achieved path-breaking success during the Golden Age of Islam, so you must forgive me for missing a few names. While speaking with my graphic designer, I explained the book's theme, and his name popped into my mind. That is when I realised *I had missed him!*

I am glad to include him in the book's first edition. The man I am talking about is another fine physician who proved many theories wrong and often criticised Greek physicians for their flawed theories and Indian physicians for their dogmatic approach towards science. He is the man who famously said, "Galen, you are wrong; this is not how the blood flows"(I have taken artistic liberty to convey what he said in my own words). And then went on to show the world the correct blood flow path in the body, especially between the heart and the lungs. And we are about to know it. If you are a physician or a doctor, jog your memory and ask if you were taught this. His name is Ibn Nafis.

Ala ad-Din Abu al-Hassan Ali Ibn Abi-Hazm al-Qarshi, known as Ibn Nafis Damashqi (1210 – 1285 C.E.), was born in a small town near Damascus called Qarsh. He was a physician and philosopher and spent most of his life in Cairo. He died in Damascus aged 80. He was also an expert in religious jurisprudence and theology. Ibn Nafis wrote an encyclopaedia of medicine called al Shamil fi -Tibb as well as several other books and commentaries, one of which is on Ibn Sina's Qanun fi-al-Tibb (the Avicenna's Canon of Medicine)

Before Ibn al-Nafis, Galen's views were universally accepted, particularly his assertion that blood passed through invisible pores in the interventricular septum. This wall separates the left and right ventricles of the heart. Galen believed blood from the right ventricle seeped through these pores into the left ventricle, mixed with air to generate "vital spirit," a life-sustaining force. This understanding remained unchallenged for over a millennium. Ibn al-Nafis, however, broke away from this tradition through keen anatomical observation and critical reasoning. While dissecting the human body—an activity he practised despite societal constraints—he observed that the interventricular septum was a solid, impenetrable structure without pores. Based on this observation, he deduced that blood could not pass directly from the right ventricle to the left. Instead, he proposed that the blood travels from the right ventricle to the lungs via the pulmonary artery, which mixes with air and then returns to the heart's left atrium through the pulmonary vein. This was the *first* known description of *pulmonary circulation* centuries before its *rediscovery* in Europe. Historians say there is no connection between Ibn Nafis's discovery and Europeans' conclusions if you believe in that!

It raises considerable doubt that European Renaissance physicians made this a standalone discovery, especially after learning the story of where his manuscript was found.

In 1924, the Egyptian physician and historian Dr Muhyo Al-Deen Al-Tatawi uncovered a manuscript of Ibn al-Nafis' work in the *Prussian State Library* in Berlin while researching Arabic contributions to medical science. Tatawi's findings were later verified and brought to global attention by Max Meyerhof, a German Orientalist and medical historian. Meyerhof published his analysis of Ibn al-Nafis' work, affirming the remarkable accuracy of his description of pulmonary circulation.

Until the rediscovery of Ibn al-Nafis' manuscripts, credit for the discovery of pulmonary circulation was attributed to European physicians such as Miguel Servet (Michael Servetus) and Realdo Colombo in the 16th century, during the Renaissance. While several papers have been written on Ibn Nafis's discovery, academics have not formally recognised his contribution. Such a shame!

In his renowned medical treatise, *Sharh al-Qanun li Ibn Sina* (a commentary on Avicenna's *Canon of Medicine*), Ibn al-Nafis presented his findings with remarkable precision. He described the heart, lungs, and pulmonary vessels in detail, emphasising the role of the lungs in *oxygenating* blood and refuting the Galenic notion of interventricular pores. Furthermore, Ibn al-Nafis hypothesised the existence of small connections, or *capillaries*, between the pulmonary artery and vein, a discovery that is credited to Marcello Malpighi's **microscopic** discovery of pulmonary capillaries in the 17th century, which was almost 400 years later. They needed a microscope in the 17th century to discover that which Ibn Nafis hypothesised with naked eyes centuries earlier!

I will list down some of his significant advancements:

Authorship of *Kitab al-Shamil fi al-Tibb* (The Comprehensive Book on Medicine):

This was his magnum opus, an ambitious medical encyclopaedia intended to surpass earlier works such as Avicenna's *Canon of Medicine*. Planned as a 300-volume compilation, it was incomplete at his death, but his completed volumes are filled with detailed medical insights. It represented a systematic effort to combine Greek, Roman, and Islamic medicine knowledge while incorporating his discoveries.

Sharh al-Tashrih fi al-Qanun (Commentary on Anatomy in Avicenna's Canon):

In this work, Ibn al-Nafis critically examined and commented on Ibn sina's *Canon of Medicine*. He provided corrections and additional insights into anatomy and physiology, including his groundbreaking ideas about the heart and lungs.

Ibn al-Nafis offered essential observations on the anatomy and physiology of the eye, clarifying earlier misconceptions and advancing ophthalmology.

He documented the relationship between the optic nerve and the brain, providing insights that prefigured later discoveries. Ibn al-Nafis stressed the importance of lifestyle factors like diet, exercise, and hygiene in maintaining health, similar to modern preventive medicine principles.

Ibn al-Nafis described the preparation and application of various drugs and herbal remedies. His work on pharmacology included the therapeutic effects of medicines, ensuring a better understanding of drug properties, dosage, and administration.

He emphasised the importance of analysing a patient's pulse and urine to diagnose illnesses, reflecting his attention to clinical observation and diagnostics.

Kitab al-Mukhtasar fi al-Hikma (The Selected Book on Wisdom): Ibn al-Nafis engaged deeply with philosophy, particularly Islamic philosophy and ethics. In this work, he addressed topics related to metaphysics, logic, and theology, showcasing his wide-ranging intellectual abilities.

Ibn al-Nafis challenged specific ideas from Greek philosophers like Aristotle, aligning his thought with more empirical methods. He believed that philosophical inquiry must be grounded in observation and reason rather than unverified speculation.

Ibn al-Nafis wrote extensively on Islamic theology, reconciling science and religion. His theological works often emphasised a rational understanding of God's creation, reflecting the balance between faith and reason typical of the Islamic Golden Age. He strongly advocated integrating scientific knowledge with theological principles, arguing that studying the natural world was a form of worship and a means to understand God's creation.

Ibn al-Nafis also explored creative writing and produced works that blended scientific knowledge with literary elements. For instance:

Fadil ibn Natiq (Theologus Autodidactus): This philosophical novel is considered one of the earliest examples of science fiction. The story involves a self-taught man living in isolation on a desert island who discovers philosophical and scientific truths about the natural world. This work was groundbreaking in its genre and reflected his belief in the harmony between reason, science, and divine revelation.

Another area that saw incredible advancement was a combination of a few fields: algebra, astronomy, geometry, and cryptography. We shall begin with discussing the man who gave the world a new field of Mathematics and is still known in the West by his Latin name, and yet few know him by his achievements of his roots. His name in Latin is Algorismi, and in reality, Al Khawarizmi!

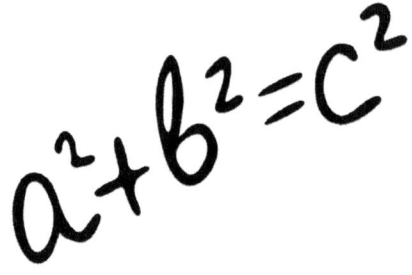

$$a^2 + b^2 = c^2$$

7

AL KHWARIZMI: FATHER OF ALGEBRA!

"If it were not for the analytical mind and the discipline of mathematics, humanity would remain in the darkness of ignorance."

– Al Khwarizmi

Muhammad ibn Musa Al-Khwarizmi (c. 780–850 CE) is arguably the standout achiever from the Golden Age of Islam. His innovations in mathematics itself are enough to place him at the higher echelons of top achievers in the world, but it is not just his contributions in mathematics he stands out for; it is also for setting foundations for other Islamic scientists to grow. He was one of the founding fathers of Al Bayt Al-Hikmah (The House of Wisdom).

Al-Khwarizmi was born around 780 CE in Khwarazm, a region in modern-day Khiva, Uzbekistan. At the time, Khwarazm was part of the excellent Persian cultural and scientific domain. The Abbasid Caliph Al Ma'mun invited him to Baghdad to lead Al Bayt Al-Hikmah, which he graciously accepted. And the rest, as they say, is History—in our case, *literally*!

In this chapter, I will discuss how he contributed to mathematics and make fleeting comments on his other significant achievements (which deserve a separate book, one which I am seriously considering).

I request your utmost patience and attention while I explain these achievements. However, it only requires you to know elementary-level algebra and geometry; you must remind yourself of the basic principles of algebra. As it is my habit to explain what things were like before Muslim scholars brought about the change, we shall continue the same approach for Algebra. Besides the obvious in the name "Al", I must say that the word Algebra is derived from the name Al Jabr from the name of his book, *Kitab al-Mukhtasar fi Hisab al-Jabr wal-Muqabala* (*The Compendious Book on Calculation by Completion and Balancing*), written around 820 CE.

Before Al Khawarizmi *taught* the world how Algebra should be solved, the Greeks merged equations with a geometric approach. Let us get straight into it. I will explain this with an example.

The Greek Way: Solving with Geometry
The Greeks didn't have equations (can you think of why? Because Al Khwarizmi was not born back then) like we do today. Instead, they imagined *shapes*. They used areas of squares and rectangles to solve problems.

Let's Solve:

$$x^2+10x=39$$

1. Start with a square:
   o x^2 Is the area of a square where each side is x.
2. Add a rectangle:
   o 10x is the area of a rectangle. One side is x, and the other side is 10.

   So now, we have:
   o A square of area x^2
   o A rectangle of area 10x.
   o Together, their total area is 39

3. Make it into a bigger square:
   o The Greeks wanted to turn this square + rectangle into one big square to make solving easier.
   o They split the rectangle into two smaller rectangles, each with an area of 5x (because 10x=2×5x, 10x = 2 times 5x).

4. Complete the square:
   o Take each 5x rectangle and attach it to two sides of the original x^2.
   o A little empty corner must be filled to complete the big square.
   o That empty corner is a small square with sides 5 (half of 10), so its area is 5×5=25.

5. Solve:
   o The big square now has a total area of 39+25=64.
   o The side of the big square is $\sqrt{64}$=8
   o The side of the original x^2 is x,
   o so: x+5=8 implies x = 3

Does all of this seem easy to you? This was the earlier complicated way of solving the equations. Now, let's see Al Khwarizmi's magic...!

Al-Khwarizmi introduced symbols and steps instead of relying on drawings. He solved the same problem $x^2+10x=39$ with logical steps:

1. Write the equation:
   Start with $x^2+10x=39$

2. Half the middle term (10x):
   o Take 10, divide it by 2, and get 5.
   o To complete the square, add 5×5=25 to both sides:
   $x^2+10x+25 = 39+25$
   o The equation becomes:
   $(x+5)^2= 64$
   Take the square root:
   o Solve x+5
   o $x+5 =+- \sqrt{64}$
   o So, x+5 =8 or x+5 = -8

3. Solve for x:
   o Solving the equation further, we get x=3 or x=-13, knowing the value cannot be negative; the answer is 3.

A quick question: did this jog your memory from school on how we were taught to solve algebraic equations by *"Completing the square"?*

This is the revolutionary method he introduced to solve algebraic equations. In hindsight, it seems insignificant, yet it was a monumental change. Al Khwarizmi changed the course of the future by introducing the *Completing the square* technique.

As seen in the example, Algebra depended on Geometry and was never recognised as an independent field in Mathematics. Khwarizmi's brilliant mind made this possible, laying the groundwork for systematic solutions of linear and quadratic equations.

Before I move on to citing his other achievements, let me explain by examples just how significant this discovery was and how it affects us in our daily lives:

1. **Engineering**
   Algebraic equations are used to model and solve problems related to structures, machinery, and systems design, e.g., Calculating the

forces acting on a bridge using equilibrium equations. In short, we can easily construct buildings because of Algebra.

2. **Economics**
   It helps analyse supply-demand curves, cost functions, and economic forecasting, e.g., Solving for a market equilibrium where supply equals demand using algebraic equations.

3. **Medicine and Pharmacology**
   Used to model drug interactions, dosages, and rates of absorption or elimination. E.g., Calculating the concentration of a drug in the bloodstream over time using rate equations. The magnitude of this is unparalleled.

4. **Physics**
   Algebraic equations describe fundamental principles like motion, energy, and electromagnetism. For example, solving Newton's second law, $F = ma$, to find acceleration. Newton might not have been able to solve it without al Khwarizmi's algebraic approach!

5. **Cryptography and Cybersecurity**
   Algebraic equations are central to encoding and decoding secure information. Algorithms like RSA encryption rely on algebraic equations involving prime factorisation. Algebraic equations encrypt your data.

   Note: RSA encryption is one of the most widely used public-key cryptographic systems, named after its inventors Ron Rivest, Adi Shamir, and Leonard Adleman, who introduced it in 1977. It is used for secure data transmission, particularly over the internet, and is a foundation of modern cryptographic protocols.

6. **Artificial Intelligence and Machine Learning**
   Algebraic equations model neural networks and optimise algorithms for, e.g., Solving for weights and biases in machine learning models using systems of equations.

7. **Astronomy and Space Exploration**
    Determines trajectories of celestial bodies and spacecraft, for, e.g., Solving Kepler's equations to calculate the orbital paths of planets. His contributions give us precise distances between planets, galaxies, and multiverse.

8. **Finance and Investment**
    Analyses risks, returns, and the value of financial instruments. For example, it Identifies the present value of future cash flows in discounted cash flow (DCF) analysis.

Below are some of his other groundbreaking contributions:

1. Introduction of Algorithms:
    The term "algorithm" originates from the Latinized version of Al-Khwarizmi's name. His methods for solving equations and performing calculations formed the basis for algorithms essential in computer science today. What I am saying here is that our computers use algorithms to function and perform every task, which is directly attributed to his contributions. To think of it, I can type my book out on the computer because of millions of algorithms running in the background, making this a reality. And I owe this to Al Khwarizmi. Spare a moment to ponder just how much this affects you and me.

2. Decimal Positional Number System
    Al-Khwarizmi's treatises on Indian numerals introduced the decimal positional number system to the Islamic world and, later, to Europe through translations. Before this, Arabs wrote numbers in words and not in numerals. This system included the concept of zero (*sifr*), revolutionising arithmetic and simplifying calculations. (Note: Zero as an idea had been known to be in use as far back as the Sumerian civilisation, so neither Al Khwarizmi nor Indian Astronomers, namely Aryabhata or Brahmagupta, discovered Zero. But this is a whole other book waiting to be written)

They laid the foundation for modern arithmetic, replacing cumbersome Roman numerals.

3.   Astronomical Contributions:
   A.   Astronomical Tables
       Al-Khwarizmi compiled comprehensive zij (astronomical tables), synthesising Greek and Indian knowledge with his observations. His *Zij al-Sindhind* included tables for calculating the positions of the sun, moon, and planets. These tables improved the accuracy of astronomical calculations and were widely used in the Islamic world and Europe.
   B.   Eclipse and Celestial Observations
       Al-Khwarizmi contributed significantly to understanding solar and lunar eclipses, and his methods were used to refine the Islamic calendar.

4.   Geography and Cartography
   A.   Revision of Ptolemy's Work
       Al-Khwarizmi corrected and expanded upon Ptolemy's *Geography*, creating maps and detailed coordinates of cities and geographical features.
       His book, *Kitab Surat al-Ard* (*The Image of the Earth*), represented the known world more accurately.
   B.   Measurement of the Earth
       He collaborated with other scholars to measure the Earth's circumference, achieving a remarkably accurate estimate for his time. However, his method was like the earlier known method of walking the dessert (Earth), which had a few challenges, which were later solved by another polymath of immense calibre and unparalleled mind named Ibn Biruni; we have discussed in detail how he calculated the circumference of the Earth with the accuracy of 99%.

Translations: In the 12th century, scholars such as Gerard of Cremona and Adelard of Bath translated his works into Latin, making them accessible to European scientists. Al-Khwarizmi's methods for solving equations and his numerical system became standard references in medieval European universities. His *Zij al-Sindhind* influenced astronomical works during the Renaissance.

Algebra became a universal language of mathematics, influencing fields such as engineering, physics, and economics. Algorithms, rooted in his work, are fundamental to computer science and artificial intelligence. This made him one of the first polymaths of The Golden Age of Islam. His zij helped many future astronomers who made incredible advancements, including Al Battani, arguably one of the biggest names to emerge during The Golden Age of Islam. He and Al Tusi directly influenced Nicolai Copernicus and his heliocentric model. How? We shall soon see that; however, let me first discuss another figure who furthered Al Khwarizmi's work and advanced it to include quadratic equations with a higher degree. Abu Kamil was from Egypt and is fondly known as the *Egyptian Calculator*.

Abu Kamil: The Egyptian Calculator

Abu Kamil Shuja ibn Aslam, often called "Al-Hasib Al-Misri" (the Egyptian Calculator), was a prominent Egyptian mathematician who lived circa 850–930 CE.

He is known for his significant contributions to algebra and for advancing the work of his predecessor, Al-Khwarizmi. Fibonacci, who gave us the Fibonacci series, was inspired by him; in fact, he copied his methods to solve equations. As we shall shortly see...

Abu Kamil expanded upon Al-Khwarizmi's foundational work in algebra, introducing methods to solve equations involving higher powers up to the eighth degree. Al Khwarizmi could solve equations up to the power of 2 or 2nd degree. He systematically incorporated *irrational numbers* as solutions and coefficients in equations, a practice not commonly accepted before his time. Why is this important? Let's see...

Before Abu Kamil, irrational numbers were primarily treated geometrically. For example, the Greeks regarded $\sqrt{2}$ The diagonal of a square with side one but hesitated to accept it as a "number" in an algebraic sense. Abu Kamil normalised their use as algebraic entities, making algebra more versatile and universally applicable.

By incorporating irrationals directly into equations, Abu Kamil shifted the focus from visual or spatial representations to precise symbolic calculations. This was a critical step toward modern algebra, where equations can represent abstract ideas independent of geometry.

Fibonacci (Leonardo of Pisa, c. 1170–1250 CE) studied Arabic mathematics during his travels in North Africa and explicitly borrowed Abu Kamil's methods in his book *Liber Abaci* (The Book of Calculation), published in 1202. Abu Kamil pioneered the inclusion of irrational numbers in algebraic equations, normalising operations involving terms like $\sqrt{2}$ $\sqrt{3}$ and their combinations. Fibonacci adopted this practice in *Liber Abaci*, using irrational numbers in a similar algebraic framework. For instance, Fibonacci solved problems where square roots appeared as coefficients or terms in equations—ideas influenced by Abu Kamil's systematic approach.

Let me give you an example of how Fibonacci used Abu Kamil's method in his equation in his book:

A problem from Abu Kamil's work asks for the solution of an equation involving the side lengths of a square where the diagonal is expressed using the Pythagorean theorem: $x^2 + x\sqrt{2} = 10$

In this case:

- x is the length of a side of the square.
- $\sqrt{2}$ Is the irrational term derived from the square's diagonal ($x\sqrt{2}$).
- The equation demonstrates Abu Kamil's ability to manipulate irrationals algebraically.

In *Liber Abaci*, Fibonacci presents a similar problem:

Find the side of a square given that the diagonal is expressed by $\sqrt{2}$ contributing to an equation involving its total length.

Fibonacci's problem-solving approach mirrors Abu Kamil's:

1. He represents the diagonal as $\sqrt{2}$.

2. He incorporates it into an equation to solve for x using algebraic manipulation $\sqrt{2}$ as a regular quantity rather than avoiding it or approximating it geometrically.

For example: $x^2 + 2x\sqrt{2} + 4 = 12$
Here,

* x^2+ is the square of the side.
* $2x\sqrt{2}$ Represents a term proportional to the diagonal.
*   Fibonacci manipulates the terms algebraically, solving for x systematically and demonstrating a continuity of the methods seen in Abu Kamil's work.

Before Fibonacci, only Abu Kamil used this method in the history of mathematics. And we are made to believe Fibonacci did this without any connection to Abu Kamil. These are some incredible facts that the majority of us Muslims have no idea of. Every single one of us has studied a chapter on Fibonacci and his famous Fibonacci series. Not once were we told that his approach to solving his equation was identical to that of a Muslim mathematician. Not once!

Whether you are from India, the USA, or Europe, I would wager that even in Muslim nations, this is little known, which is a sign of pity for us. All the while, Europeans spread the word far and wide about how they influenced modern mathematics and astronomy.

As mentioned, Muslim mathematicians and astronomers influenced Fibonacci and figures like Nicolai Copernicus in mathematics and astronomy. But now, we will see just how we did it!

In short, things are about to get intense; it is in this section where I make large claims on how Nicolai Copernicus didn't work in a vacuum and was heavily influenced, and in some way, directly copied the work of Muslim astronomers and laid the foundations to his heliocentric model.

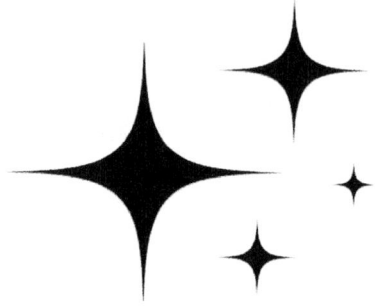

8

WRITTEN IN THE STARS AND CALCULATED BY MUSLIMS!

"The seeker of truth must, above all else, question and investigate, for knowledge is attained through reason and observation, not through blind imitation."

– Nasr Al Din Al Tusi

The history of astronomy is a testament to humanity's enduring quest to understand the cosmos. Among the most profound chapters in this journey lies the contributions of the Islamic Golden Age. During this time, astronomers of the Islamic world preserved the knowledge of ancient civilisations and revolutionised the field with groundbreaking discoveries and innovations. These advancements laid the foundation for modern astronomy and significantly influenced subsequent scientific revolutions in Europe and beyond. The astronomers of the Islamic Golden Age approached their work with a unique blend of scientific rigour, mathematical precision, and a profound sense of curiosity. This era saw the refinement of astronomical instruments, the development of new mathematical techniques, and the production of comprehensive star catalogues (Zij) that remained unparalleled for centuries. Figures such as Al-Battani refined Ptolemaic astronomy by introducing trigonometric concepts like sine, cosine, and tangent, which became indispensable tools for celestial calculations. His meticulous measurements of the *solar year* and planetary orbits corrected errors in earlier models and influenced European astronomers, including Copernicus. It is ridiculous how accurate Al Battani was in calculating the number of days in a year. Don't worry, I have discussed his entire processJ

Similarly, Ibn al-Haytham (This man is a legend! A gutsy one; see chapter 10 to know what I mean), known for his pioneering work in optics, applied empirical observation to critique and improve existing theories of celestial mechanics. His scientific method—centuries ahead of its time—reshaped how astronomical inquiry was conducted. Another towering figure, Al-Zarqali, designed the universal astrolabe, an instrument that could be used anywhere on Earth, revolutionising navigation and timekeeping. Astrolabes were highly local, and every city or area required a unique astrolabe to measure the time of the day accurately. His correction of the solar orbit's eccentricity and his astronomical tables, later translated into Latin, were studied extensively in medieval Europe. While working at the Maragha Observatory, Nasr al-Din al-Tusi introduced the "Tusi Couple," a geometric model that resolved inconsistencies in Ptolemaic astronomy and directly influenced the heliocentric theories of the Renaissance (Here is your first hint). Ulugh Beg established one of the largest observatories in Samarkand and compiled star catalogues with astonishing precision, demonstrating the enduring legacy of Islamic astronomy well into the 15th century.

Perhaps the most remarkable aspect of the Golden Age of Islamic astronomy was its global and interdisciplinary nature. Scholars from diverse religious and cultural backgrounds collaborated to push the boundaries of knowledge. They developed instruments like astrolabes, armillary spheres, and celestial globes, enabling precise observations and calculations. Their work was efficient, aiding navigation, determining prayer times, and creating accurate calendars. Yet it was also profoundly philosophical, reflecting a desire to understand the universe as a manifestation of divine order.

The impact of these advancements extended far beyond the Islamic world. Translations of Arabic texts into Latin during the 12th and 13th centuries introduced European scholars to the works of Al-Battani, Al-Zarqali, and Al-Tusi, among others. These texts became standard references in medieval European universities and played a critical role in shaping the Scientific Revolution. The meticulous observations, refined mathematical models, and innovative instruments developed by Islamic astronomers bridged the ancient and modern worlds, transforming astronomy from a *speculative art* into a **precise science**. While the intent is to present every achievement, it is outside the scope of a few hundred pages, so I will focus on a few achievements that every reader needs to know.

Al-Battani revolutionised trigonometry by introducing the sine, cosine, and tangent functions as replacements for the Greek *chord* method.

His work included:

Development of trigonometric tables with *unprecedented* accuracy, computing the values of sine and tangent functions. Introduced formulas such as: **$\sin(a+b) = \sin(a) \cos(b) + \cos(a) \sin(b).$** Defined cotangent, secant, and cosecant functions.

If you have read the book religiously until now, you would have started to remember these formulas by now. And yet, for the first time in your life, you now know these were a Muslim contribution (this, to me, is the most significant achievement of the book). These advancements simplified astronomical calculations and became foundational for *spherical* geometry and navigation.

Al-Battani made precise measurements of celestial bodies, significantly improving Ptolemaic astronomy.

He calculated the solar year's length as 365 days, 5 hours, 46 minutes, and 24 seconds (his method will be discussed soon), an improvement over Ptolemy's estimate. He determined the inclination of the Earth's axis with greater accuracy, contributing to understanding the *precession of the equinoxes (The precession of the equinoxes is a gradual change in the direction of the Earth's rotation axis, which causes the position of the celestial poles to drift through the constellations at a continuous rate of roughly 20 arcseconds per year).* His measurements influenced Islamic and European astronomers, including Copernicus, who directly referenced Al-Battani's data in his heliocentric model.

Al-Battani identified and corrected errors in Ptolemy's Almagest, a foundational text of ancient astronomy.

Improved calculations of the orbits of the sun and moon. Demonstrated that the apogee (the point farthest from Earth) of the sun's orbit is not fixed but moves over time, contributing to understanding orbital mechanics. (This was quite significant) These corrections made astronomical models more accurate, enabling precise eclipses and planetary position predictions.

The *Zij al-Sabi* (Astronomical Tables)

Al-Battani's most famous work, *Zij al-Sabi*, is a comprehensive compilation of astronomical data, methods, and trigonometric tables. Tables for calculating the positions of stars, planets, and other celestial bodies. Instructions for solving problems in spherical astronomy using trigonometry. Data for predicting solar and lunar eclipses. *Zij al-Sabi* was translated into Latin in the 12th century, influencing European astronomers such as Kepler and Regiomontanus.

Practical Applications for Navigation

Al-Battani applied his trigonometric and astronomical knowledge to improve navigation. Developed methods for calculating the qibla (direction of Mecca) based on celestial observations, which were crucial for Islamic practices. His work on spherical trigonometry was directly applicable to determining latitudes, longitudes, and routes for travellers and sailors. His advancements in navigation influenced explorers during the Age of Discovery (15-17 century when Europeans explored the world by sea), providing tools for accurate seafaring.

We shall briefly discuss these astronomers; their much more significant contributions will be discussed in separate topics.

We saw earlier that he calculated the number of days in a year as accurately as 365 days, 5 hours, 46 minutes, and 24 seconds. We will now see how he did this. Al Battani had the base, to begin with, the data he had from Egyptians and Babylonians; their estimate was 365 days, 6 hours, and 10 minutes, which you can see is not as accurate; now, to improve on this, he used an armillary sphere to measure how the length of the shadow varies over the year, and based on this, he was able to find out the day when both day and night are of the same length, in other words, the Equinox. He repeated this for **40 years, patiently,** may I add.

He had access to the Greek text that was written 700 years earlier and discovered the precise day its author also measured the same phenomenon, the Equinox; now, given the genius he was, he took into account two key points: first, the number of days between two measurements, and the number of years between two measurements. He then divided the first number by the second number and arrived at the astonishing figure of 365 days, 5 hours, 46 minutes and 24 seconds, within just 2 minutes of the actual number. He did this without any telescope, just with an Armillary sphere, astrolabe and his naked eye!*

(*Note: Excerpts taken from Jim Al Khalili's narration from the BBC Documentary names Science and Islam)

Al Battani and Copernicus:
In the University of Padua in Northern Italy lies a book written by a Polish astronomer Nicolai Copernicus named De revolutionibus orbium coelestium" (*On the Revolutions of the Celestial Spheres*), published in 1543. This is the book that brought the paradigm shift in the way we look at the celestial bodies. He shook the world by stating that all the bodies,

including planets, orbit the Sun, not Earth. In other words, the Heliocentric model. A point to note here is that the ancient Greeks believed Earth was static and everything moved around it. For a long time, there has been an assumption that there was a vacuum between the time of the Greeks and Nicolai Copernicus as if everything that Copernicus had learnt and observed came out of nowhere. And what he wrote was poles apart from what the Greeks believed. Ever thought, how could it be?

On careful reading of his book, one can easily see that he credits most of his learnings to someone he mentions as Machometi (Muhammadi) Aracenfis, who is Al Battani. I encourage you to do an exercise: look up "Carlo Alfonso Nallino," who wrote the "Opus Astronomicum", which is a general term used for groundbreaking astronomical work, which is on the astronomical work of Al Battani and his Zij, which is known as Zij Al Shabi.

Finding Al Battani's name in Copernicus's book proves that people didn't live in a vacuum between the Greeks and the Renaissance. The Islamic Golden Age formed the basis upon which he was able to build his Heliocentric model. While he only credits Al Battani by mentioning him, irrefutable evidence shows that more than one astronomer inspired him. That brings us to the master astronomer of the Maragha Observatory: Nasr al-Din al-Tusi, commonly known as Al Tusi and how the Tusi Couple directly relates to Nicolai Copernicus. Be prepared to be astonished, and this is not an overstatement!

I will be honest: when I started reading about the Golden Age of Islam, I heard different names like Ibn Sina, Al Biruni, and Jabir Ibn Hayyan, which corresponds to the magnitude of their achievements. However, I had never heard of the man named Al Tusi. I would be a millionaire if I could earn a penny for how many of you share this thought. Al Tusi deserves a special mention, as you are about to find out.

Nasr al-Din Al Tusi was born in 1201 in the city of Tus (That is how he got the title Al Tusi), in Khurasan, located in eastern Persia (Modern world Iran).

He studied theology from his father and loved delving into various subjects like logic, philosophy, and mathematics. He completed his education in Nishapur and was highly regarded as exceptional. However, Al Tusi had to make some difficult decisions, and he had to make them fast as the threat of Mongols was looming over the region, so he joined the religious movement at the time that was inclined towards the Isma'ili shia; their group had a firm hold on the Mount of Alamut (Yes, the same one that you know of from the movie "The Prince of Persia") with the group called Hashasins (Yes the same group on whom the game "Assassins Creed" is based).

There, he set up his observatory and began his work. However, it wasn't long before Mongols marched on the foothills of Mount Alamut, defeated Hashasins and gained control over the mountain. Al Tusi's life was in danger; he had to act fast and intelligent; he somehow managed to convince the Mongol leader and the grandson of Genghis Khan, Hulagu Khan, that he would add immense value and also predict the future if he was given resources to conduct his observatory research, to which the Mongols agreed and thus began the work on setting up the observatory in Maragha. Such was the reputation of Al Tusi that he attracted scholars from far and wide, as far away as China. He made significant advancements to the number system and wrote a masterpiece called The Transversal Figure (Shakl al Qita), considered the first independent book on trigonometry. Al Tusi led a group of the best polymaths to start a revolution to shape what was forthcoming: The Renaissance!

Such were his efforts that this endeavour became known as the Maragha Revolution! However, his most influential work was yet to come. Al Tusi wrote the book that, in many ways, became the fundamental book on which European astronomy was based. This book is called Tadhkira fi Ilm al-hawala, or Memoir on Astronomy. In this book, he wrote about his famous geometric construction, which came to be known as the **Tusi Couple**.

Before we jump into Al Tusi's Couple, which laid the foundations for many mechanical and engineering marvels in the future, let's see why Al Tusi proposed the Couple.

Before Al Tusi, Ptolemy's geocentric model was considered the go-to model, which described our Solar system with Earth at the centre of it. However, it had flaws; e.g., it could not explain why planets move with different speeds and, at times, appear to move backwards (retrograde motion) when observed. To explain it, he made further changes, which made his model even more questionable. He believed that all planets move on smaller circles called "Epicycles", which move around larger circles called the "Deferrents".

This explained the retrograde motion but required a convoluted, overly complex system of "nested circles." Each planet required its unique set of epicycles, making the model cumbersome, inelegant, impractical and impossible.

As discussed above, planets appear to move at different speeds when observed from Earth. To counter this, he introduced an imaginary point called "Equant," the system's centre. This meant he had to move the Earth's centre, which essentially contradicted the belief that Earth was the centre of the Universe.

To address these issues, Al-Tusi proposed a geometric innovation (the **Tusi Couple**), which elegantly resolved irregularity in planetary motion without relying on the problematic equant.

So, here it is…

The Tusi couple consists of two circles: a larger circle with another slight circle rotation within its circumference and a diameter that is half the larger circle. The smaller circle rotates twice as fast as the larger circle and in the opposite direction. **Now read carefully:** as the smaller circle rotates at a higher speed, at any two given points, it makes a straight line between the two exact opposite ends, and as it rotates, it makes multiple such consecutive lines; this motion creates the same effect as the back-and-forth oscillation of a planet observed in the sky, explaining retrograde motion without requiring additional epicycles or an equant. What is more fascinating is that he didn't just state this; he described this system geometrically and provided mathematical proofs showing that the sum of the motions of the two circles could replicate observed planetary paths.

This is what Al Tusi's couple looked like (second figure on the next page): Here are the notations: Starting from the top of the larger circle, we see Alif moving downwards along the diameter; the next is Haa, Daal (the first letter along the diameter of the smaller circle) and then Baa. On the smaller circle, moving along the diameter of the smaller circle, we see Faa followed by Jeem. English equivalents of these letters are A, H, D, B, F, and J. Now, let's look at the model proposed by Nicolai Copernicus. Every letter coincides with its Arabic counterpart in placement; in other words, you see A in Copernicus's model where Al Tusi wrote Alif, B where Baa is written and so on.

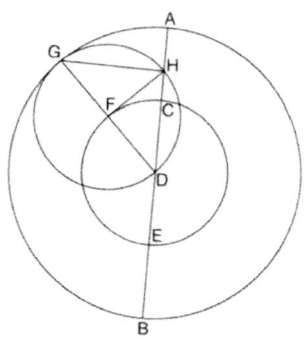

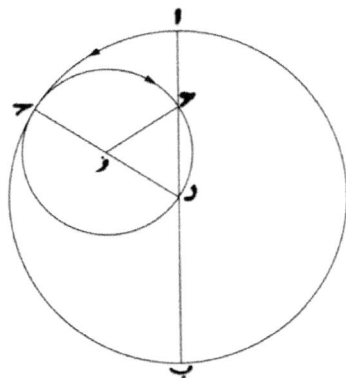

Is this a mere coincidence? Based on research studies, Copernicus copied Al Tusi's model to present his Heliocentric model of our Solar System. He was so influenced by the astronomers of the Golden Age of Islam, and his work was so heavily dependent on the observational data (Zij) from

Muslim astronomers that many scientists even believe that Copernicus was not the first astronomer of the Renaissance but the last astronomer of the Golden Age of Islam.

Let us now see how he used the Tusi Couple to prove his Heliocentric model: Nicolaus Copernicus incorporated the **Tusi Couple,** which provided Copernicus with a mechanism to eliminate the need for epicycles (small circular orbits superimposed on larger orbits) in the Ptolemaic geocentric system and helped refine his heliocentric model. In his work, Copernicus adapted the Tusi Couple in his heliocentric system to simplify planetary motion. Copernicus employed a variation of the Tusi Couple to replace the epicycles used to explain planets' oscillations and retrograde motions.

He used the Tusi Couple's ability to generate linear motion from circular motion to accurately describe planetary paths while maintaining a more straightforward mathematical structure.

The Tusi Couple also allowed Copernicus to address the problem of eccentric orbits (orbits not perfectly centred around Earth or the Sun). It enabled him to represent these orbits mathematically without needing additional epicycles. By incorporating the Tusi Couple, Copernicus further undermined the geocentric model's reliance on excessive complexity and epicycles. This strengthened the case for his Sun-centered system. At the beginning of this section, I said that irrefutable evidence was found that Tusi directly impacted Nicolai Copernicus, which is why I said that. The diagram that you saw above is directly sourced in his book, De revolutionibus orbium coelestium, and yet he never credited Tusi for it, perhaps he thought if we didn't, we would never find out. Oh Well!

Despite these groundbreaking revelations, I still applaud the work of Nicolai Copernicus as it was his work that laid the groundwork for further development of research on our Solar system;, yes, he used Tusi couple to arrive at his heliocentric hypothesis, however, he still had a lot to do and he did that, and for that he deserves all the credit he gets, all I am asking for is, the same level of respect to be shown to Al Tusi and other gigantic astronomers from the Golden Age of Islam.

All of this "astronomical" advancements were possible by one thing and One thing alone, in the modern world, we call that "A grain of doubt" It was only after *one man* decided to doubt the gigantic Almagest by Ptolemy that Islamic scholars were able to achieve groundbreaking advancements; this "grain of doubt" was the reason why we now have Heliocentric model. He wrote an entire book called Shukuk 'ala Batlamyus" (*Doubts Concerning Ptolemy*), which became instrumental in driving the thought process of the Maragha Revolution led by Al Tusi and his inspirational work. This book was written by none other than the "First Scientist" in the World, Ibn Al Haytham. Arguably the most outstanding scientist the Golden Age of Islam has produced. The mammoth figure whose name is spoken in the same breath as the name of the great Sir Issac Newton. We will talk about the "First scientist" in chapter 10, but let us conclude this chapter for now.

I will only do justice to end one chapter with the greatest astronomer who directly influenced Copernicus and begin the next with arguably the greatest polymath in the world (I don't say that lightly). The man who mapped the whole world with 99% accuracy. The man who seemingly influenced Newton through translations of his books. The man who discovered the natural tendency of objects to fall to the ground, in other words, **Gravity!**

9

AL BIRUNI AND HIS MOUNTAIN (APPLE DIDN'T FALL ON ISSAC NEWTON)

"The study of the heavens is a gateway to understanding the divine order and the vastness of creation, revealing the wisdom of the Creator in the language of the stars."

– Al Biruni

We started the previous chapter with Al Battani, one of the finest astronomers of the Golden Age of Islam and a towering figure in mathematics and astronomy. I thought of ending the chapter with another giant of the Golden Age of Islam. However, I realised he deserved a separate chapter; therefore, I edited his achievements in a separate chapter. So, let's discuss now why I named Chapter 4 **"The Greatest Polymath…maybe."**

Al-Biruni, whose full name is Abū Rayḥān Muḥammad ibn Aḥmad al-Bīrūnī, was a renowned Persian scholar and polymath and one of the most significant intellectual figures of the Islamic Golden Age. His lifetime contributions spanned diverse fields, including astronomy, mathematics, geography, history, medicine, and philosophy. Arguably the best "polymath" the Islamic Golden Age has produced, his work remains unparalleled, and some of his significant works exist even today.

Al-Biruni was born in Khwarazm (modern-day Khiva, Uzbekistan) in 973 CE. Khwarazm, located in Central Asia, was a centre of culture and learning during his time, providing an ideal environment for his intellectual pursuits. However, all was not easy for him, as his childhood was marred with unbearable challenges; his father passed away while he was very young, and his mother brought him up. Al Biruni moved from one place to another throughout his life. However, this proved to be a boon rather than a bane, as he made many discoveries during his travels, as you will see shortly.

Al-Biruni initially studied with renowned scholars in the court of the Khwarazm rulers, who valued knowledge and sponsored intellectual pursuits. He was exposed to diverse subjects, including astronomy, mathematics, medicine, philosophy, and natural sciences, which became the foundation for his career across various disciplines, earning him the title of a "Polymath."

One of his primary mentors during his formative years was Abu Nasr Mansur, a prominent mathematician and astronomer who introduced Al-Biruni to the works of classical Greek scholars such as Euclid, Ptolemy, and Archimedes. Under Abu Nasr's guidance, Al-Biruni delved deeply into geometry, trigonometry, and spherical astronomy, mastering these disciplines to a level where he began innovating on existing theories. During this period, Al-Biruni also studied the Arabic translations of Greek texts preserved and enhanced by earlier Islamic scholars.

Al-Biruni showed an early interest in philosophy and metaphysics. His education included rigorous training in Islamic theology and law and exposure to Zoroastrianism and other pre-Islamic Persian philosophies still prevalent in Khwarazm. This intellectual diversity allowed him to approach knowledge with an open mind, a trait that characterised his later works.

Al Biruni and Ibn Sina were contemporaries who often found each other on the opposite side of the spectrum, usually disagreeing on various topics. Al Biruni wrote several letters to Ibn Sina, and Ibn Sina responded to his early letters; however, later, he thought it was a waste of his time and relegated the job to his secretary. Their letters are fascinating in discussing several aspects of metaphysics and philosophy.

The political turmoil in Khwarazm during Al-Biruni's youth disrupted his studies. Around 995 CE, a rival faction overthrew his patrons, forcing him to leave his homeland. During this exile, he travelled to the Samanid court in Bukhara, another significant learning centre, where he likely encountered scholars deeply engaged in Persian and Indian scientific traditions. His early studies in Bukhara included advanced mathematics, astronomy, and possibly Sanskrit, a language he would later master to study Indian texts.

It was quite a revelation when I learned that he is not as famous as some other scientists from the Golden Age of Islam, though his work is considered some of the most groundbreaking for his time. To point out a few of his achievements would be to do injustice to his other spectrum of work; however, I will have to do this injustice to Al Biruni to draw your attention to just how great his mind was, but before I do so, let me shortly tell you about some of his achievements.

Ibn Biruni was known to write books on history. During his extensive travels, he documented phenomena and his observations. One such book he wrote was dedicated to his patron, Qabus. "The Chronology of Ancient Nations" is regarded as one of the most outstanding books on medieval history.

He also wrote a book on India, The History of India, named "Ta'rikh al-Hind," which is considered a primary source of information by many historians, Indians and foreigners.

In 1017, Al-Biruni was invited to the court of Sultan Mahmud of Ghazni (some accounts state he was abducted), where he became a court scientist and scholar. Mahmud's conquests of India allowed Al-Biruni to accompany the Sultan on expeditions. During these travels, he extensively studied Indian culture, science, and religion. He mastered Sanskrit and translated Indian texts into Arabic, bridging the knowledge gap between the Islamic and Indian civilisations.

During these travels, he did something still considered a medieval marvel: He measured the circumference of the Earth to within 1% of its actual value without telescopes or modern equipment, just with his eye and an astrolabe. So, how did he do it? That is the one story we shall discuss, as I believe it is nothing short of a miracle! But before that, as is famously known, the most accurate calculation was done by Eratosthenes, which was less than 1% of the actual value, so why is Ibn Biruni's method considered more accurate?

The method applied by Eratosthenes and all others (Including Muslim astronomers) before Ibn Biruni involved mapping the earth via footsteps; for this to work, he took two points on the Earth separated by a vast distance. He sent people from Syene to Alexandria, about 800 miles away. I will quote Jim al Khili here and borrow his explanation from his book "The House of Wisdom: How Arabic Science Saved Ancient Knowledge and Gave Us the Renaissances":

"But the truth is that Eratosthenes was very lucky to have got so close. There were a number of serious errors, inaccuracies and crude guesses involved in his method that conspired by chance to give an answer so close to the correct one." He then adds, "Most importantly, it would not have been possible to measure the distance between the cities with any degree of accuracy at all. Counting paces would have been unreliable and the path taken would in all likelihood have followed meandering course of the Nile, including complex Delta region around Alexandria. Lastly, we do not know the exact length of his unit of distance, *the stadion*; he then adds, "The fact that number of paces came to exactly 5,000 stadia is suspicious, and most modern historians do not believe Eratosthenes ever did have the distance measured this way."

Note: He used *the stadion* as the unit of measurement, which was considered standard at the time like we have feet, metres, kilometres etc. One *stadion* was the length of the Greek stadium. However, the length of the stadium was different in Egypt and Greece.

Ibn Biruni was sure that he could calculate the circumference of the earth; in fact, in his book, he starts with his famous line, "Here is another method for the determination of the circumference of the Earth. It does not involve walking the desert" (Ibid; p 183). Geography was the only thing stopping him from doing so. Let me explain. Al Biruni needed a certain kind of topography that didn't exist in the Arab world; he needed a mountain and a valley. He found just the right topography while travelling to India with Ghazni.

What I am about to share should surprise you, if not shock you. If there is one story from this book that you pick up to share with your friends, it should be this. During his travels, he identified a place called Nandana in modern-day Pakistan. He climbed atop the hill to get a clear view of the plane, which was necessary as he wanted an unobstructed view of the horizon.

He needed the height of the mountain first to put the trigonometric and algebraic calculations together. So, the way he calculated the mountain's height is nothing short of a genius; he took two observational points from the plain, which needed to be in a straight line. He then measured the distance between those two lines. Let us visualise it.

Al Biruni picked two points in the line of sight of the mountain; let's call the first point "a" and the second point "b." The angle measured from these points is a shown b (shown in the following figure). Now, from the first observation point (a), he measured the angle a from the ground to the mountaintop with the help of an astrolabe. He then moved farther away to the following observation point (b) and repeated the same process to determine the angle b.

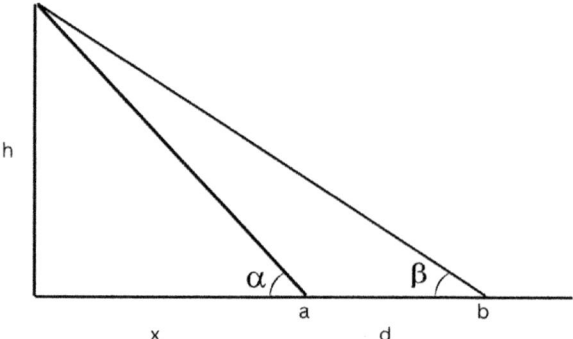

Now, he applied a simple tangent function (with basic knowledge of trigonometry, you will understand it).

Imagine a triangle where the mountain's height (h) is the vertical side, and the distance from your observation point to the mountain's base (x) is the horizontal side.

The tangent of an angle (tan) is:

$$\tan (\text{angle}) = \frac{Height\ of\ the\ mountain(h)}{Horizontal\ distance(x)}$$

Now, applying this formula at the observation point "a", we get:

$$\tan(\alpha) = \frac{h}{x}$$

Rearrange it further:

$$x = \frac{h}{\tan \alpha}$$

Now, going further at point "b", since we are farther away, let us call this distance between a and b "d".

Now, applying the same to the second observational point, we get:

$$x+d = \frac{h}{\tan \beta}$$

Now, we combine both equations.

$$x = \frac{h}{\tan \alpha} \text{ and } x+d = \frac{h}{\tan \beta}$$

Substitute the value of x from the first equation in the above equation; we get:

$$\frac{h}{\tan \alpha} + d = \frac{h}{\tan \beta}$$

Now, one needs to know basic math to solve for h, and we get:

$$h = \frac{d.\tan(\alpha).\tan(\beta)}{\tan(\beta) - \tan(\alpha)}$$

Now that the height of the mountain had been determined, he used another trigonometric formula (elementary level) to determine the radius of Earth.

Al-Biruni recognised that the dip angle of the horizon is directly related to the curvature of the Earth. By visualising a right triangle formed by the mountain, the centre of the Earth, and the visible horizon, he applied a geometric relationship to determine the radius of the Earth. The key equation that could be used is as follows:

$$\sin (\text{dip angle}) = \frac{height\ of\ the\ mountain}{radius\ of\ earth + height\ of\ the\ mountain}$$

He further simplified it to arrive at the equation:

$$\text{Radius of Earth} = \frac{height\ of\ the\ mountain}{\sin (dip\ angle)}$$

Once he got the radius, he applied the formula Circumference = 2p*r

Post reading the equation, you should have two questions, first: why did we remove the *height of the mountain* Post simplifying the equation, here is the simple answer to the question: it is because the height of the mountain is negligible as compared to the radius of Earth, so can be ignored, second question: If it can be ignored, why did have to climb it at the first place and calculate it?

This is where the Genius of Biruni shines; I will explain this with an example: Consider a giant ball, of the size of a swimming pool; if you stand at the same level as the ball's surface, you will not be able to see the complete sphere that the ball is, whereas, if you climb two floors and then look at the ball, you will see a much larger surface area, that is why he had to climb the mountain so that he could get a much clearer view of the horizon. The height of the mountain is essential in the initial equation, as the angle of the dip depends on it.

I hope this made sense

Al Biruni was 99% accurate using this method, described in the book Determination of the Coordinates of Cities. His estimate was 24,668 miles, and the current known value is 24901 miles.

Al Biruni was a masterclass in himself; he was considered the first-ever anthropologist in the world. He explicitly wrote about "gravity" in his book, *Al Qanun Al Masudi* (The Masudi Canon). In the book, he talks about the *natural tendency* of any object to fall towards the centre of the Earth. Though he didn't coin the word Gravity, this was a stunning discovery; his studies on the circumference of the Earth and the shape of the Earth naturally led to his thoughts on why objects move downward, towards its centre, as the Earth is spherical. With extensive translation, his books reached Europe, and therefore Issac Newton, and yet we are told to believe "The apple fell on Issac Newton" that made him discover "Gravity"!

These achievements call for special recognition, which he never got. These are the reasons (and many more that I could not mention) why I say it is a close call between Ibn Sina and Ibn Biruni on who should be the best polymath.

If it were my call, I would go with Ibn Biruni. We conclude the chapter with the first ever written record of the concept of *Gravity,* the man who influenced Issac Newton (arguably) and begin the next with another man who directly influenced Issac Newton, in his own words, I might add, this time in a far more significant proportion as you are about to find out. The first scientist the world has ever produced. The man who changed the way *Light* is perceived. The man who defined the field of optics, the man who taught *the way of science* to the world. As stunning and controversial as it may sound, you won't have to wait long to read my reasoning and the substantiation of these big claims.

10

FIRST SCIENTIST IN THE WORLD

"The duty of the man who investigates the writings of scientists is to examine everything critically and not to accept it simply on the writer's authority. To doubt and question is the first step toward wisdom."

– Ibn Al Haytham

I concluded the previous chapter controversially by addressing Ibn Haytham as the First Scientist in the world. Let me begin this chapter by addressing the Elephant in the Room: was Ibn Al Haytham the first scientist in the world? If so, what about all those who preceded him? We are not talking about lab shrimps or Pico physicists here; we are talking about mammoth figures like Galen, Aristotle, Ptolemy, Eratosthenes, etc. So, let me lay it bare to you. All these great names were *theorists*; while they did derive excellent formulae and gave us astronomical data, they needed a systematic scientific method to conclude rigorous testing and experimentation. Their methods were philosophical, observational or theoretical, not *demonstrative*! Whereas Ibn Al Haytham formalised a scientific process, he thought that observational data is "a mere starting point" and that we must test these observations with various permutations and combinations and that we should be able to arrive at a consistent result.

He believed in empirical evidence and emphasised that experiments should be repeatable and verifiable by others, not just one person, which is the backbone of modern science. He believed in conducting controlled experiments with different data points (Variables) to test a hypothesis. The visionary work began by asking a fundamental question, "Kaifa Nadhara" (*How do we see*)? And so did he, like no other before him, ironically in a dark cell where he was held captive by the Caliph in Egypt.

Abu Ali Al Hassan Ibn al Haytham was born in 965 CE in Basra, present-day Iraq, a hub of cultural exchange within the Abbasid Caliphate. Ibn Al Haytham came from a middle-class family that emphasised pursuing formal education. Ibn Al Haytham was exposed to classical Arabic literature, the Holy Quran, and grammar. He was naturally curious, so he pursued Mathematics, Theology, Astronomy, and Optics. Ibn Al Haytham, while studying Almagest by

Ptolemy quickly figured out the flaw in his model (as discussed earlier) and was frustrated by the fact that the entire structure needed to be revised. Hence, he decided to take up a project pointing out flaws in the Almagest; of course, his contemporaries laughed at him. However, they soon came around and accepted what he wrote. This book he called Shukuk 'ala Batlamyus" (*Doubts Concerning Ptolemy*) became a textbook that encouraged next-generation scientists and astronomers to advance in their respective fields.

Ibn al Haytham's reputation started to spread far and wide; such was his reputation that he received a personal invitation from the Caliph of Egypt, Al Hakim Bi Amr Allah, to create a dam on the river Nile. He readily accepted; however, upon arrival in Cairo, he soon realised the Nile and its flooding could not be tamed, and he expressed his inability to perform the task, which the Caliph didn't take well and ordered his execution. Ibn Al Haytham fiend madness and the Caliph decided to put him under house arrest for several years. However, some records state that he was placed under house arrest to begin with. And this is where it all began! Ibn al Haytham started writing about his findings in optics while in an asylum. Some of Kitab Al Manadhir's greatest works must have started while in confinement, as we get this book in 7 volumes, and it is nothing short of an absolute marvel. His work is considered at the same level as the book by Sir Issac Newton, "Principia Mathematica", which is why, in the previous chapter, I referred to him as being equal to none other than Newton. Newton famously said, "If I have seen further, it is by standing on the shoulders of giants." I wonder who he is referring to. One obvious response is that he might have been referring to Greek scholars; my argument is that he was referring directly to Ibn Al Haytham, and let me make my substantiation. Ibn Al Haytham is called the father of Scientific methods; Newton adhered to this method and furthered it. The point to note is that no Greek scholar followed the scientific method. The only literature written on light and optics of this sheer magnitude before Newton was Kitab Al Manadhir by Ibn Al Haytham; Issac Newton expanded his work on light. Ibn al Haytham was the first person to explain the intromission theory correctly; Newton used that exact theory to expand his work on optics; do you see where this is going? Facts cannot be hidden for long. They are out in the bare now!

Ibn al Haytham and Greeks' Emission theory:
This is a fascinating story; shockingly, Greek scholars had various theories about Vision, meaning how we see. Euclid and Ptolemy believed that our eyes emanate rays that reflect from the object and hit us back, enabling

us to see; I know this makes no sense, but this is what they believed. Aristotle, on the other hand, believed in the intromission theory, with a caveat, which is light enters our eyes from the object we are looking at, and here is the caveat; instead of believing that light is reflected from the surface of the object, he felt the space between the object and our eyes is illuminated. If you thought this was messed up, wait till you read the next point. Plato and Galen combined Emission and Intromission (with the above caveat) to state that our eyes emit rays that reflect from the object's surface, illuminated by the space between the object and our eye, enabling us to see. Give it a thought: our eyes emit rays of light, meaning our eyes are the source of light, and if that is to be the case, why do rays need to reflect from any surface and then return to the eyes for us to see? Why can't we just…"see"? And this is what Ibn Al Haytham thought and quite frankly ridiculed the above theories.

Instead, he used a mathematical approach to prove the intromission theory, stating that *"light from an object reflects, travels in a straight line, and hits the eye, enabling us to see"*. This theory is now known as the *"theory of vision."* And it was this theory that was expanded upon extensively by later optics, including, you know who! The great Sir Issac Newton.

Moon Illusion:
Have you ever wondered how the Moon near the horizon appears extremely large but pretty small up in the sky? Earlier Greek scholars thought this was because of magnification caused by the earth's atmosphere. However, it was Ibn al Haytham who said it is merely psychological as there is nothing up in the sky to compare the size of the moon to; e.g., near the horizon, one can see it behind trees or aligned with a mountain since we know how big the mountain is, we can relate it with the size of the moon, but in the sky, there is no relatable body. This is called "Moon Illusion," and Ibn al Haytham was the first person to explain it.

Camera Obscura:
While Ibn Al Haytham made incredible advancements, Camera Obscura is the most famous. There are various stories about how he discovered it, made it work and how phenomenal it was at the time. Some stories

say that he was in confinement still where he saw the light enter the cell through a pinhole that made him wonder if our eyes emit rays, how is it possible that I cannot see anything in the cell if I cover the pinhole and that there has to be another source of light, which we now know as **The Sun**. Nevertheless, Ibn Al Haytham decided to experiment; he went about creating a small box that was hard covered on three sides with a pinhole on one side and a cloth on the opposite side (4th side); he let the light enter the box only through that pinhole, what he observed shook him as much as it did everyone else around him. There was a reflection of the object on the 4th side (the side opposite to the pinhole), meaning light entering through the pinhole was reflected on the surface, creating an image of the object from which it had been reflected; however, it was *inverted*! And there is a reason why the image appears inverted.

Let me attempt to explain it in simple words. Light travels in all directions but always in a straight line unless it changes the medium. Light travelling from vacuum to water will change its direction and then continue in a straight line in the changed direction. So, if the medium is constant, light will keep travelling in a straight line in all directions infinitely; now, imagine a tree; light reflecting from the surface of the tree will travel in every single direction, meaning light that is travelling in linear direction, will continue to do so, light travelling from the top of the tree diagonally downwards will continue to do so, similarly, light from the bottom of the tree travelling diagonally upwards will continue to travel in the upward direction. If this is clear, let us apply this to the Pin hole Camera Obscura; except the pinhole opening, everything else is covered, meaning most of the rays will be blocked, and only light travelling from the top of the tree downwards will enter the pinhole, and continue travelling downwards, and light from the bottom of the tree, continue travelling upwards, with multiple rays travelling towards the cloth on the 4th side through the pinhole, create an inverted image of the tree. So, to answer the question, Ibn al Haytham asked, *"This is how we see!"*

Ibn al-Haytham was a prolific author. He wrote over 200 works on a wide range of subjects, of which at least 96 of his scientific works are known, and approximately 50 of them have survived. Nearly half of his surviving works are on mathematics, 23 are on astronomy, 14 are on optics, and a few are on other areas of science. Not all his surviving works have yet been studied, but some of his most important ones are described below. These include:

- *Kitab Al Manadhir* (Book of Optics)
- *Risalah fi al-Dawa'* (Treatise on Light)
- *Mizan al-Hikmah* (Balance of Wisdom)
- *Maqalah fi al-Qarastun* (Treatise on Centers of Gravity)
- *Risalah fi al-Makan* (Treatise on the Place)
- *On the Configuration of the World The model of the Motion of the Seven Planets*

His book Kitab Al Manadhir is divided into seven volumes and covers various aspects of optics. I will discuss something trivial, yet it will prove that he was the first to develop spectacles (eyeglasses) that enabled people with impaired vision to see.

Ibn al-Haytham was the first to describe the convex lens's ability to converge light rays. He observed that when light passes through a convex lens, it bends towards the focal point, producing a magnified image. This phenomenon was groundbreaking as it explained why particular objects appeared larger when viewed through curved glass.

Ibn al-Haytham used polished, transparent materials like glass and crystal to create lenses. By shaping these materials into convex forms, he demonstrated their capacity to focus and magnify light. His experiments involved shining light through these lenses onto a surface, where he observed how the light rays converged to form a brighter, clearer image.

Through these observations, Ibn al-Haytham identified the relationship between the curvature of the lens and its magnifying power. A steeper curvature resulted in greater magnification, a principle later applied to develop powerful magnifying glasses and spectacles.

By refining the shape of convex lenses, Ibn al-Haytham effectively created the first magnifying glass. He demonstrated that convex lenses could enlarge small text or objects, aiding those with poor vision. This marked the beginning of practical optics for vision correction, a field that would evolve significantly in later centuries.

Knowing eyeglasses were only developed in the 13th century, hundreds of years after Ibn Al Haytham showed the world that objects can be magnified with precise and careful use of convex lenses, was nothing short of astonishing.

And he didn't just say it or write a geometrical formula about it; he proved it. Ibn al-Haytham pioneered meticulous experimental techniques involving controlled scientific testing to validate theoretical hypotheses and support inductive reasoning. His scientific approach closely resembled the modern scientific method, following a cyclical process of observation, hypothesis development, experimentation, and independent verification. He would repeat the process several times, including hypothesis and experimentation, and emphasise the need for verifying his processes independently.

I have left hints at various placed in the book, easter eggs that give you an idea of what topics I would write my forthcoming books on; one of the strong contenders who deserves a separate book dedicated to his work would be undoubtedly Ibn Al Haytham, and until the book arrives, we will have to limit our extent of discussion till here, I hate to do it, however, if I continue, I might not stop. Such was the stature of this man, who directly and substantially influenced the works of Isaac Newton and his optics; he is rightly called the most outstanding optic in 2000 years between Issac Newton and Archimedes. And yet, the masses don't know about him as he deserves. It is up to us not to forget that the *"First scientist in the world was a Muslim!"*

As children, we were fascinated by focusing a beam of light through a glass surface onto a piece of paper, watching in awe as it caught fire. Little did we know that this phenomenon had been mathematically explained for the first time in history by a man named **Ibn Sahl** in his treatise *On the Burning Instruments*. This remarkable work was lost for centuries and rediscovered in the 1900s in two separate locations, Damascus and Tehran. **Rushdie Rasheed** painstakingly brought these fragments together and wrote a paper on them. Little did he know there lay a hidden treasure within this rediscovered manuscript: the **Law of Refraction of Light**—a law historically attributed to **Willebrord Snell,** who proposed it in 1621.

In this discussion, I will argue that this law should rightfully be called Ibn Sahl's Law, as he accurately described it 600 years before Snell. The Law of Refraction of Light has far-reaching implications in our daily lives. It enables the creation of contact lenses, helps determine the purity of liquids (such as the amount of water mixed with milk), and ensures the precise formulation of drugs, safeguarding patients from overdoses. It is fundamental to countless applications in physics, enabling research into the universe, the discovery of distant galaxies, and the search for life on other planets.

It also profoundly impacts the lives of people on Earth through technologies that rely on the precise manipulation of light. Despite the immense significance of this law, most of us remain unaware that it was first discovered and mathematically formulated by a Muslim scholar. Such recognition would correct historical oversight and honour the contributions of Ibn Sahl, whose genius continues to shape our world today. I know by now, you have a *burning* desire to know what this law is; what if I tell you every student learns this in high school? Would you be surprised? Nevertheless, here is **the law of the Refraction of Light.**

The Law of Refraction of Light describes how light bends when it passes from one transparent medium to another with a different refractive index. In simpler words, The Law explains how light bends when it passes from one material to another, like from air into water or glass. This bending happens because light travels at different speeds in different materials. The law is represented mathematically as below:

$$\frac{\sin(\theta)1}{\sin(\theta)2} = \frac{n1}{n2} \text{ (constant)}$$

In other words, $\frac{\sin(\theta)1}{\sin(\theta)2}$ is always constant.
Where,

1. n1: Refractive index of the first medium (air).
2. n2: Refractive index of the second medium (water).

3. θ1: Angle of incidence (measured between the incident ray and the normal to the surface).

4. θ2: Angle of refraction (measured between the refracted ray and the normal to the surface).

$$\frac{\sin(\theta)1}{\sin(\theta)2} = \frac{n1}{n2} \text{ (constant)}$$

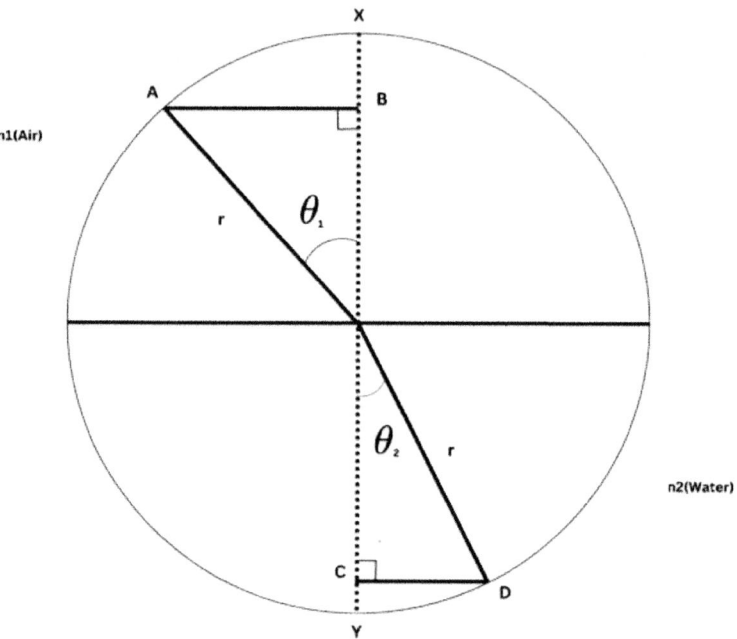

In the above diagram, as per Ibn Sahl $\frac{AB}{CD}$, it is always constant. Now, we need to show that $\frac{AB}{CD}$ it is equivalent to $\frac{\sin(\theta)1}{\sin(\theta)2}$. For this, we use the sine law from trigonometry, which states that "the sine of any angle is the ratio of the side opposite the angle to the hypotenuse." In other words, sin (q)1 = $\frac{AB}{r}$ and sin(q)2 = $\frac{CD}{r}$. Now, all we need to do is divide sin(q)1 by sin(q)2, which gives us the below equation:

$$\frac{\sin(\theta)1}{\sin(\theta)2} = \frac{AB/r}{CD/r}$$

Solving the equation further, both r cancel out, we get,

$$\frac{\sin(\theta)1}{\sin(\theta)2} = \frac{AB}{CD} \text{ (constant)}$$

Hence proved!

What makes this even more remarkable is that Ibn Sahl described this relationship almost 600 years before Snell. While this is acknowledged and recognised in academic circles, the question remains: Will the scientific community officially rename this Ibn Sahl's Law? Unfortunately, that seems unlikely. However, this does not change the historical reality. We must know his contributions and give credit where they are due.

Advancements in mathematics not only furthered the development of optics but also greatly affected the growth of mechanics. The Golden Age of Islam saw the rise of mechanical devices that would give the world Internal Combustion Engines. In other words, we can drive cars, buses, and ships essentially because of the engineers of the Golden Age of Islam. Did you know that? Engineers of the Golden Age of Islam are responsible for developing the modern world's water pump, irrigation, and water supply systems in urban areas. One prominent name that stands out in Engineering is Al Jazari, from designing the first automata to setting the standard for irrigation systems. He is the subject of many great discussions in the field of mechanics, and he is the protagonist of our next story.

11

HIS MACHINES COULD SERVE
FOOD AND WATER

"Ingenuity is the path to solving the problems of life, for the beauty of invention lies in its ability to turn ideas into reality."

– Al Jazari

One of the most prominent names that we must highlight is Al Jazari. Badi' al-Zaman Abu al-'Izz ibn Isma'il ibn al-Razzaz al-Jazari, commonly known as Al-Jazari, was a 12th-century polymath, engineer, and inventor who revolutionised the fields of mechanical engineering and hydraulics. Born in 1136 CE in Jazirat ibn Umar (modern-day Cizre, Turkey), Al-Jazari lived during the height of the Islamic Golden Age. His birthplace, situated near the banks of the Tigris River, was part of the Artuqid Dynasty, a region known for fostering intellectual growth and technological innovation. Little is documented about his early life, but Al-Jazari likely benefited from the scholarly atmosphere of the court of the Artuqid kings, who were his primary patrons.

Al-Jazari's most significant contribution to engineering is his monumental treatise titled "Kitab fi Ma'rifat al-Hiyal al-Handasiyya" (*The Book of Knowledge of Ingenious Mechanical Devices*), written in 1206 CE. This manuscript is a manual of over 100 mechanical devices and groundbreaking work that blends scientific rigour, practical applications, and artistic creativity. Al-Jazari meticulously illustrated his inventions in the treatise, providing detailed descriptions and assembly instructions, making it a precursor to modern engineering manuals. His work demonstrates a profound understanding of mechanics, hydraulics, and the use of materials, and it was intended not only for practical utility but also as an intellectual pursuit.

Al-Jazari's most iconic inventions were his water clocks, marvels of engineering and artistry. Powered by flowing water, these clocks were designed to measure time accurately while incorporating elaborate mechanisms and automata for visual appeal. The Elephant Clock, for example, featured a complex system of weights, levers, and water flow, along with cultural symbols from India, Persia, Greece, and China, reflecting Al-Jazari's cosmopolitan outlook. This clock was not merely a timekeeping device but also a symbol of the interconnectedness of civilisations through science and art. Another example of his ingenuity was the Castle Clock, a massive water-powered device capable of marking the passage of time, showcasing celestial movements, and even adjusting automatically for the length of day and night.

Al-Jazari also made significant advancements in hydraulics, particularly in developing water-raising devices. His designs for water pumps included innovative features such as the double-action suction pump, which utilised reciprocating pistons to draw water more efficiently. This invention was a precursor to modern pump technologies and was crucial for irrigation and urban water supplies. Al-Jazari's work on water wheels and automated systems also demonstrated his deep understanding of fluid dynamics and mechanical principles, which he applied to solve practical problems in agriculture and city planning.

One of Al-Jazari's most remarkable contributions was his work on automata, mechanical devices that mimic human or animal actions. These included programmable humanoid robots, such as a servant who could pour water to wash hands, and musical automata capable of playing melodies on drums and flutes. These creations highlighted his technical prowess and creativity in designing machines that entertained and inspired awe. His ability to combine function with form set him apart as a true pioneer in engineering. Al-Jazari's genius extended to developing mechanisms that have become foundational in modern machinery. He is credited with inventing the crank-slider mechanism, which converts rotary motion into linear motion, a principle later applied in internal combustion engines (Engines that drive our vehicles). He also refined the use of gears, cams, and valves, integrating them into devices that were centuries ahead of their time. His work laid the groundwork for many mechanical systems driving modern technologies. The significance of Al-Jazari's contributions go far beyond his era. His treatise was translated into multiple languages, and his inventions influenced Islamic and European engineering. His work bridged the gap between ancient mechanical traditions and the innovations of the Renaissance. European inventors, such as Leonardo da Vinci, drew inspiration from Al-Jazari's designs, underscoring his global impact on the history of technology.

Al-Jazari's legacy is not just one of mechanical innovation but also of blending art, science, and culture. His machines were functional yet aesthetically pleasing, reflecting the Islamic Golden Age's emphasis on beauty in scientific endeavours. Al-Jazari's meticulous documentation of his inventions ensured that his knowledge would endure, providing a valuable resource for generations of engineers and scientists. He passed away in 1206 CE, the same year he completed his magnum opus. While Al Jazari is a noted figure in the field of mechanics, we cannot say the same about the three Banu Musa brothers. So, let me highlight how significant their achievements were shortly, no matter how trivial. But first, let me talk about the "Gravity" of the elder brothers' achievement. He wrote a treatise named "Astral Motion and the Force of Attraction", which talks about a force acting on the celestial bodies that were the same as the force we observe on Earth, in other words, Gravity! It was unprecedented to talk about Gravity half a century before Newton (Including Al Biruni, as seen in chapter 9). Together, the Banu Musa brothers on their famous automated fountain, self-regulating oil lamps; they spoke of the automated fountain in their treatise *Kitab al-Hiyal* (*The Book of Ingenious Devices*); the fountain could maintain varying water levels and create dynamic water displays without manual intervention. Their idea behind it is pretty remarkable and yet simple.

The fountain had two concealed reservoirs: one for water and another for air. When water was released from the primary reservoir, it created pressure in the air chamber, pushing water through pipes and into the fountain. A series of weighted floats and counterweights controlled the flow of water. As water reached a specific level, the float would rise and trigger a valve to close, halting the water flow. Similarly, when the water level dropped, the valve would reopen to restore the flow, maintaining a consistent level. The design allowed water to spurt at varying heights and patterns, creating a functional and aesthetically pleasing ornamental display. The Banu Musa's oil lamp was another ingenious device designed to adjust the oil flow automatically to maintain a steady flame. This invention addressed a typical issue of the time: the difficulty of keeping a consistent light source without frequent manual adjustments.

While Ibn al Haytham failed to build a dam on the Nile, Al Farghani succeeded in measuring the river's flow. This was essential for predicting floods and planting crops. The device, called a Nilometer, has remained in use for centuries. The Nilometer consisted of a vertical column or a series of graduated steps installed in a water well or basin connected to the river. Al-Farghani refined its design to improve accuracy by incorporating precise calibrations based on astronomical and hydraulic principles. The mechanism relied on observing the rise and fall of the Nile's water, marked against a fixed scale engraved on the column or steps. This allowed seasonal flooding to be monitored, enabling predictions about irrigation needs and crop yields. Al-Farghani's contributions helped refine the system's reliability, ensuring better management of Egypt's agricultural economy, a critical aspect of the region's prosperity.

Any chapter on mechanical engineering and innovations would only be complete, mentioning the first man to take flight, whose name is etched on the moon. The man who was intellectual enough to design a flying machine 600 years before Issac Newton, crazy enough to launch himself from a mountain peak at 65 to demonstrate that he could fly, the first aviator in recorded history, Abbas Ibn Firnas.

Abbas Ibn Firnas was born in Ronda, Malaga, in 810 CE, less than 200 hundred years after the death of the prophet, and to think he achieved such jaw-dropping success in that period is quite inspiring. He was an ardent astronomer. He constructed an elaborate planetarium in Córdoba that simulated celestial movements. This device demonstrated the positions and motions of planets and stars, providing a valuable tool for astronomical education. The planetarium also included mechanisms to simulate weather phenomena like thunder and lightning, reflecting his engineering prowess. Ibn Firnas built precise astronomical instruments to study celestial bodies and timekeeping. His work influenced the development of astrolabes and other tools that advanced Islamic and European astronomy. Ibn Firnas designed and improved Water Clocks; he is credited with creating a more sophisticated hydraulic clock that used water to measure time. Ibn Firnas was a glassmaker; he contributed to techniques that advanced glass-making in Andalusia. He was instrumental in creating clear glass, which was later applied to producing lenses for reading and astronomical instruments. His work in glassmaking paved the way for advancements in optics, a field further developed by scholars like Ibn al-Haytham, though this point is widely debated.

However, what is not disputed is that he flew at 65(some records state he was between 65 and 70). Let us dive into that story now.

The story of his historic flight begins with rigorous preparation. Observing birds in flight, Ibn Firnas studied the mechanics of their wing movements, how they caught the wind, and how their tails provided balance. He sought to replicate these natural phenomena through engineering. Using silk, wood, and feathers, he constructed a large glider that mimicked the structure of bird wings. The silk fabric served as the surface of the wings, while the wooden frame provided the necessary rigidity. Feathers were added to enhance the aerodynamic properties of the device. Ibn Firnas understood that this gadget would need to harness the air to generate lift, even if he needed help to articulate the modern principles of aerodynamics fully. The launch site was a hill near Cordoba named Rufasa, chosen for its elevation and open space, allowing for a sustained glide. A crowd gathered to witness this audacious attempt, their excitement tempered by uncertainty. Ibn Firnas, clad in his glider-like apparatus, took his position on the hilltop. He extended the wings outward, preparing to leap into the unknown. The onlookers held their breath as he ran forward, gaining momentum, and then launched himself into the air.

To the astonishment of those present, the glider lifted off the ground, and Ibn Firnas soared through the air. Historical accounts suggest that he remained airborne for a significant distance, skillfully manipulating the wings to maintain his glide. This was no mere leap—it was a controlled flight. The crowd watched in awe as he demonstrated the feasibility of human flight, defying the limits of the era's understanding of motion and engineering. However, the flight had its challenges. As Ibn Firnas approached the end of his glide, the absence of a stabilising tail—an element he had observed in birds but had not incorporated into his design—caused the glider to become unsteady. He struggled to maintain balance and landed heavily, injuring his back in the process. Despite the imperfect landing, Ibn Firnas survived the attempt, and the lessons he gleaned from his experiment became the foundation for his later reflections on flight mechanics.

Following the flight, Ibn Firnas analysed the shortcomings of his design with remarkable excitement and scientific rigour. He identified the lack of a tail-like structure as the primary reason for the instability during landing. This insight demonstrated his ability to learn from experimentation and to adapt his designs based on empirical evidence. His recognition of the importance of balance and control in flight was a precursor to the principles that would govern aviation centuries later. While there are no records of subsequent flight attempts by Ibn Firnas, probably due to the injury he sustained while landing, also as he died within 7-12 years of this flight, his experiment left an indelible mark on history. It was a bold, unprecedented step toward realising the ancient human dream of flight. His work predated Leonardo da Vinci's famous designs for flying machines by centuries. And foreshadowed the scientific breakthroughs that would eventually lead to powered flight.

Imagine taking flight in the 9th century, at least 500 years before the next attempt to **design** a flying machine could be created. I said attempt to design, **not to create**. For his early design of the flying machine, he later came to be known as "Da Vinci of Andalusia" Though Ibn Firnas never got the recognition that Da Vinci got and still has, he was one of the forefathers of mechanical flights. NASA named a crater on the Moon after him for his incredible aviation, optics, and mechanical engineering achievements.

12

AL KINDI TAUGHT US HOW TO CONCEAL WRITING

"We ought not to be ashamed of appreciating and acquiring the truth, no matter from what source it emanates. For him who seeks the truth, nothing is of higher value than the truth itself."

– Al Kindi

Abu Yusuf Ya'qub ibn Ishaq al-Kindi (c. 801–873 CE), often called the "Father of Cryptography," made significant contributions to the science of encryption and codebreaking during the Islamic Golden Age. His pioneering work defined modern cryptography, particularly his development of frequency analysis to decipher encrypted texts.

Development of Cryptography by Al-Kindi
Context and Motivation
Cryptography became increasingly important in the Islamic world for secure communication, especially in political, military, and religious contexts. Al-Kindi's interest in solving problems systematically led him to approach cryptography as a scientific discipline, blending mathematics, statistics, and linguistics.

Key Contributions:
The Manuscript on Deciphering Cryptographic Messages:
Al-Kindi authored a groundbreaking treatise titled *Risalah fi Istikhraj al-Mu'amma* (*A Manuscript on Deciphering Cryptographic Messages*), the earliest known work on cryptanalysis.

Understanding the Arabic Language:
He recognised the importance of the frequency of letters in a given language, particularly Arabic, for codebreaking. He analysed common letter pairings and the structure of Arabic words, such as the frequent use of definite articles (*al-*).

Frequency Analysis: Al-Kindi's Formula for Breaking Codes
How It Works:
Al-Kindi developed frequency analysis, a method for breaking substitution cyphers (ciphers). It involves analysing the frequency of letters in the ciphertext and comparing it to known letter frequencies in the language.

1. Understanding Letter Frequency:
    In any given language, certain letters occur more frequently than others. For Arabic, Al-Kindi identified that letters like *alif*, *lam*, and *mim* are more common, while others appear less frequently.

Steps in Al-Kindi's Codebreaking Process:
o Step 1: Count Frequencies:
   ▪ Tally how often each letter appears in the ciphertext.
o Step 2: Compare Frequencies:
   ▪ Compare these frequencies to a known frequency distribution of letters in the Arabic language.
o Step 3: Substitution:
   ▪ Substitute the most common ciphertext letters with the most frequent letters in Arabic.
o Step 4: Contextual Analysis:
   ▪ Refine substitutions using linguistic knowledge and context, identifying common words like *Allah or Muhammad* or grammatical markers.

Mathematical Representation:
The basic principle of frequency analysis relies on probability:

$$P(L) = \frac{Frequency\ of\ letter\ L\ in\ ciphertext}{Total\ letters\ in\ ciphertext}$$

Where P(L) is the probability of a letter L in the ciphertext, which is compared against the expected frequency in the language, let us understand this with an example:

Below is the ciphertext, and our goal is to reach a readable plain text:

XLI MHIR MW RSX E CERI

Step 1: Look at the Ciphertext
         The message seems like a messy code. A secret rule has replaced each letter with another letter.

Step 2: Count the Most Frequent Letters
         We count how many times each letter appears in the message:

Letters	Frequency
I	3
M	2
X	1
L	2
E	2
R	2
S	2
T	1
C	1
N	1

Step 3: Compare with Common English Letters
In English, the most common letters are:

- E, T, A, O, I, N, S, R

The most frequent letters in our code are I, M, L, and S.
We guess:
- I → E (since "E" is the most common letter in English).
- M → T (another frequent letter in English).

Step 4: Start Decoding
Replace I with E and M with T in the ciphertext: The above ciphertext changes to as written below:

XLE TEHR EW NOT E TENE

Step 5: Look for Common Words
The word TEHR needs to be clarified. What if T is A?

Let's change T to A:

XLE AEHR EW NOX E AENE

Now, EW could be the word IS. That means E → I and W → S.

Step 6: Refine Further
After substituting these new letters:

XLI AIRH IS NOT I SINE

The phrase starts making sense! Now, XLI could be THE, so:

- X → T
- L → H
- I → E

After replacing all the letters based on our guesses, the decoded message becomes:

THE BIRD IS NOT A CAGE

Please note that these are based on the fundamentals of frequency analysis. Then, they would use their logic and understanding of the language to replace letters via permutations and combinations to arrive at the final result.

How Al-Kindi's Method Works:

1. Count letters in the coded message to find the most frequent ones.
2. Match them to the most common letters in the English language (E, T, A, etc.).
3. Use patterns of common words (like THE, IS, AND) to refine the decoding.

Of course, he did this in Arabic, using the letters of the Arabic Alphabet and their respective frequencies. Nevertheless, this was quite impressive for that age.

Applications of Al-Kindi's Cryptanalysis

1. Deciphering Messages:
   o Governments and military leaders in the Abbasid Caliphate used them to decrypt enemy communications and protect sensitive information.

2. Advancements in Secure Communication:
    o   Al-Kindi's work laid the groundwork for more secure encryption methods by highlighting vulnerabilities in substitution cyphers.
3. Influence on Later Cryptography:
    European cryptographers later adopted and expanded his principles during the Renaissance and beyond.

Experiments were not just conducted in cryptography; several experiments and demonstrations were also conducted with various metals, often to obtain the ultimate form of metal: Gold!

This field came to be known as alchemy. Several prominent figures explored it, but only a few applied science to it. The most notable among them was Jabir Ibn Hayyan, more commonly known as Geber in the West. Jabir was the foremost person in the world to establish a field known as ***chemistry***! He was a prolific chemist who loved his lab and showed us how to purify water. Yes, it was he who gave us *Distillation*. We will talk about him in the next chapter

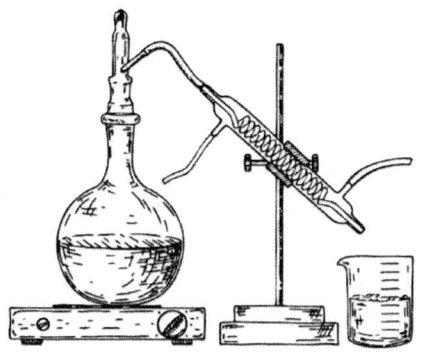

13

MAGIC IN THE CHEMISTRY
LABORATORY OF THE ALCHEMIST

"The first essential in chemistry is that you must perform practical work and conduct experiments, for he who merely theorises about the natural world without testing it is like a man who stares at shadows and seeks the truth from them."

– Jabir Ibn Hayyan

Jabir Ibn Hayyan: Real Father of the Modern Chemistry

Being a student in the field of science, I feel ashamed of myself. I just learned about the man who invented an entire stream in the field of science, Chemistry! At times, I wonder if I had known about him while experimenting on distillation; perhaps my life would have been a little prouder, knowing that he was from the Golden Age of Islam. Nevertheless, this is why I began writing this book, so our next generation knows this while working in the field of Chemistry...And if you are not someone who has ever dealt with chemistry, I welcome you to this revelation that will leave you shell-shocked, and if you are from the Western world, this will be a good wake-up call about the Golden Age of Islam. Give it a thought; you and I drink clean water, "distilled" from all impurities because of a Muslim! Every single day. Oh, this might gaslight millions!

It almost seems impossible that two of the most influential stalwarts of the Golden Age of Islam were imprisoned at some point in their life, Ibn Al Haytham and Jabir Ibn Hayyan, however, at different times, as we will shortly see. Jabir ibn Hayyan, known in the West as Geber, is one of the most iconic figures of the Islamic Golden Age. Born around 721 CE in Tus (Yes, the same city that Al Tusi was born in), a city in present-day Iran, Jabir is widely regarded as the father of modern chemistry due to his monumental contributions to alchemy and his pioneering efforts in transforming it into what we now recognise as Chemistry. Before Jabir, the world considered this a mystical tradition, attributing everything to the imaginary object known as "The Philosopher's Stone." Although reasonable evidence shows that people before him practised with several elements to see if they could change the structure of a component to create a new element, these were just ancient practices and not an established field of science. His work bridged mystical alchemical traditions with systematic experimentation, laying the foundation for modern scientific inquiry.

Jabir lived during the Abbasid Caliphate. He was closely associated with the House of Wisdom in Baghdad. Jabir was a disciple of Ja'far al-Sadiq, a prominent theologian and scholar and the caliph's grand vizier, Al Rashid, who profoundly influenced his approach to philosophy and science. This mentorship shaped Jabir's unique perspective on integrating empirical observation with metaphysical reasoning. Jabir's scientific contributions emerged in the broader context of Islamic thought, encouraging the pursuit of knowledge as a divine imperative. The Quran and prophetic traditions emphasise reflecting on the natural world to understand God's creation. Inspired by this ethos, Jabir sought to uncover the principles governing matter and its transformations, ultimately redefining the field of alchemy.

The Corpus of Jabir: Writing the Table of Elements
Jabir's body of work, often called the Jabirian Corpus, includes over 3,000 treatises. This is highly questionable as it is humanely impossible to write 3000 treatise. Many of these texts are believed to have been written by later followers using his name. The most significant texts attributed to him include *The Book of Balances*, *The Book of Seventy*, and *The Great Book of Mercy*. These works demonstrate an extraordinary depth of understanding and offer a glimpse into Jabir's systematic approach to categorising elements and compounds. While the commoner, when grabbing a piece of land, thought of it as dirt, Jabir considered it a composition of multiple elements coming together to form this "Dirt." Jabir was famous for being obscure, and this stems from an old belief that knowledge is sacred and should not fall into the hands of the unworthy; this may be the reason why he wrote writings that were very hard to follow, in fact here is something exciting, the word "Gibberish" comes from his Latinised name, Geber, meaning, "That which Geber wrote" indicating to the unclear and obscure writings. Jabir is also credited with naming this field of science as Al Kimiya, which was later changed to Chemistry. His seminal work is called Kitab Al Kimiya (The Book of Chemistry). Jabir's most revolutionary contribution was his attempt to organise the known elements into a systematic table. Long before Dmitri Mendeleev's periodic table, Jabir divided substances into three primary categories based on their properties:

* Metals: Substances like gold, silver, copper, and lead.
* Non-metals: Materials such as sulfur and mercury.
* Minerals: Compounds like salts and alums.

Jabir believed that all matter was composed of the classical elements—fire, earth, water, and air—but he expanded this idea by introducing the concept of chemical properties. He suggested that metals differed because of varying proportions of sulfur (representing combustibility) and mercury (representing metallic properties). This sulfur-mercury theory was a precursor to later understandings of chemical reactions and bonding. (I encourage you to search for the Sulfur-Mercury theory and how it affected our modern knowledge.)

Jabir's Methods and Innovations:
What set Jabir apart from earlier alchemists was his insistence on empirical experimentation. Jabir emphasised the importance of observation and reproducibility, unlike his predecessors, who relied heavily on mystical and symbolic interpretations. He meticulously recorded his experiments, including detailed descriptions of processes such as distillation, crystallisation, sublimation, calcination, and evaporation. These methods are still fundamental in modern chemistry laboratories. For example, Jabir perfected distillation, creating sophisticated alembics to purify liquids. This technique allowed him to extract *ethanol*, paving the way for its use in medicine and other industries. His work on sublimation led to the purification of mercury and sulfur, while his calcination studies demonstrated how metals could be broken down into their essential components. Jabir also introduced quantitative analysis, emphasising the need for precise measurements in chemical experiments. He believed that substances could be manipulated and transformed through carefully controlled processes, termed the "balance of properties." This notion was central to his idea of achieving chemical equilibrium, a precursor to modern stoichiometry.

Jabir ibn Hayyan's work marked a clear divergence from traditional alchemy. Traditional alchemy was steeped in mysticism and focused primarily on the philosopher's stone, a mythical substance believed to transform base metals into gold and grant eternal life. While Jabir operated within this framework to some extent, his approach was fundamentally different. He sought to demystify alchemy, transforming it into a systematic and evidence-based discipline.

Jabir viewed alchemy as a philosophical pursuit that aimed to understand the hidden properties of matter. However, he believed that practical chemistry—a term he used to describe the tangible manipulation of substances—was equally important. For Jabir, the goal of chemistry was not just to produce gold but to uncover the natural laws governing the material world. He referred to this as "scientia practica," or practical science, emphasising the utility of chemical processes in medicine, metallurgy, and industry.

Jabir's contributions to chemistry are numerous and groundbreaking: Acids and Bases: Jabir was the first to isolate strong acids such as nitric acid, hydrochloric acid, and sulfuric acid. These discoveries were critical for later developments in both industrial and academic chemistry.

Aqua Regia: He discovered a mixture of nitric acid and hydrochloric acid capable of dissolving gold, which he termed "aqua regia" (royal water).

Alchemy to Pharmacology: Jabir's studies of minerals and compounds significantly influenced early pharmacology. He developed techniques to synthesise medicinal compounds, including anaesthetics and antiseptics.

Laboratory Equipments:
Jabir invented or refined much of the laboratory apparatus still in use today, such as the alembic, retort, and crucible. Jabir's last days were spent in house arrest as his main patron and mentor, Ja'afar, was executed by the caliph to reduce his clan's influence on the administration of the caliphate. Jabir ibn Hayyan's impact on science extended well beyond the Islamic world. In the 12th century, his works were translated into Latin, becoming essential reading for European scholars during the Renaissance. "Geber", a Latinized version of his name, became synonymous with advanced alchemical knowledge. European alchemists, such as Roger Bacon and Albertus Magnus, drew heavily from his texts, often needing to fully understand the sophistication of his methods. For example, Jabir's emphasis on experimentation and observation influenced the scientific methods developed by later figures like Robert Boyle and Antoine Lavoisier. Boyle, often considered the "father of modern chemistry,"

acknowledged the foundational role of Islamic scholars like Jabir in shaping his understanding of chemical processes.

Another field closely related to chemistry is, of course, minerals and plants; in other words, Botany. Islamic scholars in the Golden Age of Islam furthered and refined earlier research, making many amazing discoveries. One such name is Abu Hanifa Ahmad Ibn Daud Al Dinawari.

Abu Hanifa Ahmad ibn Dawud Al-Dinawari (828–896 CE) was a Persian polymath and one of the most outstanding scholars of the Islamic Golden Age, whose contributions spanned botany, astronomy, mathematics, geography, and history. His most significant and enduring legacy lies in his pioneering work in botany, where he earned the title of the "Father of Arabic Botany." Born in Dinawar, a town near present-day Kermanshah, Iran, Al-Dinawari was part of a society deeply rooted in agricultural traditions and surrounded by diverse plant life, which likely influenced his early interest in the natural world. A product of the scholarly environment fostered by the Abbasid Caliphate, Al-Dinawari studied in prominent intellectual centres such as Basra and Kufa, where he mastered subjects ranging from linguistics to the natural sciences, blending practical observations with theoretical knowledge.

Al-Dinawari's magnum opus, Kitab al-Nabat (*The Book of Plants*), is considered one of the most important contributions to botany in the medieval Islamic world. He systematically classified and described plants in this groundbreaking six-volume encyclopedia, making it the first comprehensive botanical work in Arabic literature. His approach to the study of plants was uniquely empirical, drawing on direct observation and agricultural practices. He meticulously recorded over 600 plant species, detailing their physical characteristics, habitats, growth patterns, and practical uses. His interdisciplinary approach set Al-Dinawari apart; he integrated botany with agricultural science, medicine, and ecology, offering a holistic perspective on the natural world. For instance, he provided detailed descriptions of crops such as wheat, barley, and flax, explaining their planting cycles, soil preferences, and economic significance, which had direct applications for improving agricultural productivity.

Al-Dinawari's work also delved into the ecological relationships between plants and their environments. He studied how soil type, climate, and water availability influenced plant growth, laying the groundwork for early environmental science. His observations were not limited to theoretical descriptions; they had practical applications in improving farming techniques and understanding the ecological factors critical to sustaining agriculture in arid and semi-arid regions. His recommendations for crop rotation and soil conservation reflected a deep understanding of sustainable agricultural practices, vital for the prosperity of the Islamic world's agricultural economy. In addition to his contributions to botany, Al-Dinawari's expertise extended to pharmacology, where he identified the medicinal properties of various plants. He documented their uses in treating ailments, aligning his work with the broader tradition of Islamic medicine. For instance, he wrote about the healing properties of aloe vera, henna, and myrrh, which remain relevant in traditional medicine today. His descriptions included instructions for preparing herbal remedies and their applications in curing common ailments such as fevers, wounds, and digestive disorders. By integrating botany with medicine, Al-Dinawari bridged the gap between natural science and healthcare, making his work invaluable to physicians and pharmacists of his time.

Al-Dinawari was also a linguist and philologist, which added depth to his botanical studies. He recorded the Arabic names of plants alongside their synonyms in other languages, such as Persian and Syriac, creating a rich repository of botanical terminology. His linguistic expertise ensured that his work could be widely understood and served as a bridge between diverse cultural traditions. This multilingual approach preserved the knowledge of earlier civilisations and facilitated dissemination across the Islamic world and into Europe, where it influenced later botanical studies.

Beyond botany, Al-Dinawari significantly contributed to astronomy, mathematics, and geography, underscoring his versatility as a scholar. In astronomy, his observations on celestial bodies and their movements informed the Islamic understanding of timekeeping and calendar systems, which were essential for agricultural planning and religious observances. His work in mathematics included studies on arithmetic and geometry, which he applied to solve practical problems in agriculture and engineering. In geography, he compiled detailed descriptions of the physical and cultural landscapes of the Islamic world, offering insights into the interconnectedness of natural and human systems. The legacy of Al-Dinawari's work is profound and enduring. His empirical methods and systematic classification of plants established a model for later scientists, both in the Islamic world and beyond. His contributions to sustainable agriculture and ecological science directly impacted improving food security and resource management in regions dependent on farming. His work was translated and disseminated during the European Renaissance, influencing scholars such as Linnaeus, who later developed the modern system of *plant taxonomy*. Al-Dinawari's interdisciplinary approach, which combined empirical observation with practical applications, exemplified the spirit of the Islamic Golden Age, where science and knowledge were deeply integrated with societal needs.

In the modern world, Al-Dinawari's emphasis on sustainability and ecological balance resonates powerfully with contemporary efforts to address climate change and environmental degradation. His holistic understanding of the relationship between plants, soil, and climate offers valuable lessons for sustainable agriculture and conservation. Furthermore, his work underscores the importance of preserving traditional knowledge systems, which often contain insights critical to addressing today's global challenges.

Another noted botanist who significantly impacted the world was Abu Muhammad Abdallah Ibn Ahmad Ibn al-Baitar; his last name means "Veterinarian". Al Baitar catalogued over 1400 substances in his comprehensive work named *Kitab al-Jami fi al-Adwiya al-Mufrada* (*The Comprehensive Book on Simple Drugs*), 300 of which were his original work, not previously documented. His work with Willow bark to reduce inflammation and pain is a precursor to *Aspirin*. At the same time, his documentation of aloe vera for wound healing and skin care remains relevant in contemporary dermatology. His studies on cinnamon, cloves, and black pepper, for example, enriched their use in cooking, medicine, and preservation.

In his era, Ibn al-Baitar's understanding of antiseptic properties in plants like myrrh and camphor profoundly affected hygiene and public health practices. These insights improved medical care and contributed to the broader societal emphasis on cleanliness, a value deeply rooted in Islamic tradition. His meticulous classification of substances laid the groundwork for modern pharmacopoeias, and his interdisciplinary approach integrated botany, pharmacology, and medicine into a cohesive scientific discipline. His works were widely translated into Latin during the European Renaissance, becoming standard references in medical schools and significantly influencing European scholars like Paracelsus and Linnaeus.

Ibn al-Baitar's influence extended to the global stage, with his systematic documentation of substances providing a model for future scientific endeavours. Many of his studied plants were later incorporated into the "Linnaean taxonomy", cementing his legacy in modern botany. His work also aligned with contemporary interests in sustainable and plant-based medicine, as he emphasised the therapeutic potential of local flora. Substances like senna, ginger, and turmeric, which he analysed in detail, remain integral to alternative medicine today. Ingredients such as rose water and aloe vera, which he documented, are staples in modern skincare and cosmetics. At the same time, the analgesic effects of willow bark paved the way for the development of painkillers (as seen earlier). Ibn al-Baitar's contributions to pharmacology and botany were not confined to theoretical knowledge; they had profound practical implications for daily life. His documentation of opium as an analgesic revolutionised pain management, while his studies on spices improved the flavour and preservation of food, enhancing both health and quality of life. He recognised the economic importance of plants like saffron and nutmeg and contributed to the prosperity of agricultural and trade networks across the Islamic world.

My intention behind writing this book is to bring forth every aspect of the Golden Age of Islam, and this does not end with the Scientific Conquest; we did so much more in the fields of Geography, Arts and Architecture. And I intend to further my work by adding these in the next part. Chapters that follow are a novelty for any book written to date on this topic. That is probably the most substantial reason why I wish to highlight these achievements, from the breathtaking architecture of Alhambra to the inspiration that led to the construction of the 7th wonder of the world, The Taj Mahal. Arabic Calligraphy also played a crucial role in preserving the manuscripts of the Golden Age of Islam. Although some might consider this as a dying art, it was something that patrons loved in the medieval era. I am now happy to see the interest in Arabic Calligraphy and other Islamic art resurfacing among the young and old. And I feel a tad bit proud in contributing to that, having taught Arabic Calligraphy (Thuluth, Kufi Mushafiya, Kufi Banae) to over 3000 students in the last 7 years, many of whom went on to become instructors in their own right, while others decided to take up the mantle of becoming canvas artists adorning the walls of countless people worldwide.

In geography, we designed the most accurate Map of the world, used real gold in Illumination art, and carved structures that most would consider impossible for that age. But we did it, and you need to know!

14

THE TALE OF LAILA AND MAJNUN

"I am in Layla and Layla is in me; I cannot separate my soul from her essence, nor my heart from her love."

– Qays ibn al-Mulawwah

Islamic art can be further divided into a few ventricles; to keep it detailed yet crisp, we will dedicate chapters on Poetry, Calligraphy, other Islamic art, and Architecture. While poetry and prose were prominent even during the "Jahiliya" period, the pre-Islamic period, poetry and prose saw significant development and refinement during the Golden Age of Islam. Perhaps the terms Laila and Majnun, "One thousand and One Nights"(Arabian Nights) would ring a few bells. These were written way before the advent of the Golden Age of Islam. Nevertheless, it tells you how Arabic poetry has impacted the world. If I may indulge you in some historical facts, Majnun was, in fact, a living person who was a renowned poet himself, named Qays ibn al-Mulawwah and the story, while most of it later developed with depth in characters being portrayed by various poets during the time coinciding with the Golden age of Islam, is true!

This story is from 7th-century Arabia. The poet Qays ibn al-Mulawwah fell in love with Laila and wanted to marry her. However, Laila's parents disapproved of this and married her to someone else. This broke his heart, and he became Majnun (Madman in Arabic). It is said that even Laila was not happy with her marriage and died of heartbreak, and Majnun died at her grave upon hearing the news of her death. This, of course, is an oversimplified version of the story. However, many poets have rewritten this story, adding much-needed depth and character. The story was adapted from several cultures, including Persian and Indian cultures. A Persian poet, Nizami Ganjavi (1141–1209), was among the foremost people who added this story to his Khamsa (a collection of five poems). Amir Khursrao (1253–1325) was the poet who brought this story to the Indian subcontinent. Subsequently, many movies were written that told the couple's tale, but I am sure you know that already!

Arabic and Persian poetry was based on Love and Passion, Philosophy and Mysticism, Nature and Beauty (as the poet saw), Praise, and Satire. They were often expressed in the form of Mu'allaqat, Ruba'i and Qasida. Mua'llaqat being the most extended forms, usually spanning pages, these were the poems that were characterised by the depth of the story the poet wanted to tell, and often, his mettle was considered based on how profoundly he wrote his Mua'llaqat. I tasted this while studying for a Master's in Arabic Language (you should know I dropped out).

Al Mutanabbi (915-65) was considered the most prominent poet and regarded as one of the best poets Arabs have ever produced. He was known to be arrogant and thought himself above all else, often quoting that even the blind can see him and the deaf can hear him, expressing his capabilities. Perhaps this arrogance made him claim Prophethood, hence the lakab (moniker) Al Mutanabbi (which comes from the word Nabi). For this, he was imprisoned by the Abbasid Caliph; later, however, he was released as he renounced his prophethood. His name, however, is Abu al-Tayyib Ahmad ibn Husayn. He was born in Kufa, Iraq.

Al-Mutanabbi's poetry is best known for its qasidas, which showcase his mastery of Arabic poetic tradition. His works often celebrated the virtues of courage, pride, and ambition while lamenting human weakness and fate. Many of his qasidas were composed to praise patrons, most notably Sayf al-Dawla, the ruler of Aleppo and a celebrated military leader. Al-Mutanabbi served at Sayf al-Dawla's court, writing some of his most famous verses, combining praise with reflections on heroism and identity. However, his relationship with Sayf al-Dawla soured, leading Al-Mutanabbi to wander through various courts in search of new patrons, a common practice for poets of the time. One of his famous qasida is named "If You See the Lion's Canines", a poem about bravery and warning against cowardice, which perhaps became famous after his death. Some accounts state he was attacked by the bandits and was killed by them; it is said that the bandits were reciting his poem about bravery, all the while mocking him for being a coward. That was an irony!

Another noted poet of this era, who lived between 1207 and 1273, was Jalal al-Din Muhammad Rumi, or just Rumi as he is famously known in world history. His work revolves around love, spiritual journeys, and unity. Rumi was born on September 30, 1207, in Balkh, present-day Afghanistan, but historically part of the Persian Empire. His family was deeply rooted in Islamic scholarship; his father, Baha al-Din Walad, was a renowned theologian, preacher, and mystic. This intellectual and spiritual upbringing profoundly shaped Rumi's later works. When Rumi was young, his family fled Balkh to escape the Mongol invasions sweeping Central Asia. After wandering, they settled in Konya, part of the Seljuk Sultanate of Rum (in modern-day Turkey). This migration exposed Rumi to various cultures and ideas, including Persian, Arabic, and Turkish traditions, enriching his intellectual and spiritual horizons. Rumi spent most of his early life talking about religion, often quoting the Hadith and Quran in his work. However, his life changed once he met Shams Al-Din Tabrezi. He thought we needed to find the divine beyond books and practices; this challenged Rumi, which would eventually become the foundation of their mystic journey, hence his poetry. However, this relationship didn't last long as Shams Al-Din disappeared abruptly, which caused Rumi to go into depression.

Rumi wrote a collection of Ghazals and Rubayat for Shams Al-Din, known as Divan-e Shams-e Tabrizi. This diwan contains the famous line, "What you seek is seeking you."

Rumi wrote many works; one of his pioneer works is "Masnavi-i Ma'navi (The Spiritual Couplets). This magnum opus consists of 6 books and over 25000 verses. Some people say this is Quran in Persian for Sufi saints. This is a point that I strongly disagree with, as every devout Muslim would. However, these couplets (rhyming two-liners) are considered the best masterpieces in poetry. Here are a few translated into English:

"You were born with wings; why prefer to crawl through life?"

"Don't be satisfied with stories, how things have gone with others. Unfold your myth."

"The lamps are different, but the Light is the same. One matter, one energy, one Light, endless emanations."

"Knock, and He'll open the door. Vanish, and He'll make you shine like the sun. Fall, and He'll raise you to the heavens. Become nothing, and He'll turn you into everything."

"The wound is the place where the Light enters you."

His work can never satisfy one; perhaps that is why he has a blind following in the modern world.

15

ISLAMIC ARCHITECTURE AND ART

"Perhaps there never was a monument more characteristic of an age and people than the Alhambra; a rugged fortress without, a voluptuous palace within; war frowning from its battlements; poetry breathing throughout the fairy architecture of its halls."

– Washington Irving

Islamic Architecture:

Mosques of the medieval period were not only marvels of architecture but also reverberated the sounds of far-reaching Islamic influence on the outside and amplified the sound of the Imam (the one who leads the prayers) on the inside, without any external amplifiers; the Imam's voice was able to reach thousands praying behind them, which remains a testament to their clairvoyance and architectural brilliance. This is mainly because these Mosques, when built, were relatively smaller and later expanded, sometimes even thrice the original size, to accommodate the growing Muslim population. (Note: Smaller does not mean they were small by any extent of imagination; they were mammoth structures; what I mean by relatively smaller is, when compared to their existing size).

We begin with two unique architectural marvels that do not belong to the Golden Age of Islam. One was built before the advent of the age, and the other was built centuries after the end of the Golden Age of Islam. One inspired many mosques of the Golden Age of Islam, and the other marks the culmination of the highest achievement of Islamic Architecture. The first is the Dome of the Rock, and the second is the Taj Mahal.

The Dome of the Rock, located in Jerusalem, is one of the most iconic and earliest masterpieces of Islamic architecture, completed in 691–692 CE during the reign of the Umayyad Caliph Abd al-Malik ibn Marwan. This architectural and spiritual marvel was constructed on the Temple Mount (Haram al-Sharif), a site of immense religious significance to Muslims, Jews, and Christians. For Muslims, the site marks the location of the Prophet Muhammad's Isra and Mi'raj (Night Journey and Ascension to Heaven). Abd al-Malik commissioned the construction of the Dome of the Rock to establish an Islamic presence in Jerusalem. The construction was supervised by Raja ibn Haywah, a theologian from Beisan, and Yazid ibn Salam, an architect from Jerusalem, who were likely supported by Byzantine-trained artisans and craftsmen familiar with Roman and Persian styles. The monument was completed within approximately six years, reflecting the Umayyads' ambition to assert their political and religious authority over the region.

114

The structure features an octagonal base surrounding a circular drum that supports the golden dome, gilded initially with gold leaf, though later reconstructed with copper and gold. The dome, a stunning 20 meters in diameter and rising 35 meters above the foundation, is a visual metaphor for the heavens and the divine. The exterior is adorned with blue and turquoise tiles, which were added during the Ottoman restoration in the 16th century under Suleiman the Magnificent, replacing earlier mosaics. The interior features a richly decorated ambulatory that encircles the Foundation Stone, the central focal point of the structure. The walls and ceilings are intricately decorated with mosaics, marble, and Quranic inscriptions, many of which emphasise Islamic monotheism and the role of Muhammad as the final prophet. The inscriptions include phrases from Surah Al-Isra (17:1) and Surah Maryam (19:33–35), highlighting the continuity of Islam with Abrahamic traditions while asserting its unique theological identity.

One of the most striking aspects of the Dome of the Rock is its ability to integrate various architectural and artistic influences into a distinctly Islamic form. The Byzantine mosaics, with their gold backgrounds and vegetal motifs, reflect the artistic expertise inherited from the Eastern Roman Empire. At the same time, the structure's emphasis on symmetry, geometric precision, and the absence of figural imagery aligns with the developing aesthetic of Islamic art. The octagonal design and centralised dome would later inspire Islamic architecture across the empire, influencing the construction of mosques and mausoleums, such as the Great Mosque of Damascus and the Taj Mahal.

Furthermore, the Dome of the Rock served as a political statement, symbolising the Umayyads' dominance over Jerusalem at a time when they sought to consolidate their power against rival factions such as the Byzantines and the Shi'a Fatimids.

Over the centuries, the Dome of the Rock has undergone numerous restorations and renovations to preserve its splendour. In the 11th century, Caliph Al-Zahir, from the Fatimid dynasty, undertook significant repairs after an earthquake damaged the structure. In the 16th century, Suleiman the Magnificent ordered a comprehensive refurbishment, including replacing the original mosaics on the exterior with the vibrant ceramic tiles visible today. More recently, Jordan has overseen conservation efforts, including the re-gilding of the dome in the 20th century. Despite these modifications, the Dome of the Rock has retained its original Umayyad essence, inspiring awe among pilgrims, scholars, and architects. Rulers from different eras have invested in maintaining this marvel, which is heart-inducing. Today, the Dome of the Rock remains a focal point of Islamic identity and is a UNESCO World Heritage Site.

The Great Mosque of Córdoba, located in the heart of Andalusia, Spain, is one of Europe's most remarkable monuments of Islamic architecture. Its construction began in 784 CE under the patronage of Abd al-Rahman I, the first Umayyad Emir of Córdoba, and continued over two centuries with successive expansions by his successors. Abd al-Rahman I envisioned the mosque as a testament to his authority and the sophistication of his new emirate, echoing the grandeur of the Great Mosque of Damascus, which his family had left behind in Syria after the Abbasid overthrow of the Umayyad dynasty.

The mosque's construction was monumental and blended Roman, Visigothic, and Islamic architectural elements. Abd al-Rahman, I employed local artisans who were familiar with Visigothic and Roman building techniques. The most striking feature of the mosque's initial design was its hypostyle prayer hall, consisting of rows of double-tiered arches made from alternating red and white voussoirs, creating a visually striking effect. These arches, supported by over 850 columns of jasper, onyx, and marble, allowed for an open and airy interior space, symbolising the infinite nature of Allah. The prayer hall's orientation toward the qibla (direction of Mecca) was emphasised by the elegant simplicity of its original mihrab.

Successive rulers of Córdoba expanded and embellished the mosque, each leaving their mark. Abd al-Rahman II initiated the first significant expansion in the 9th century, extending the prayer hall to accommodate the growing Muslim population. The most important addition came during the reign of Al-Hakam II (961–976 CE), who transformed the mosque into a masterpiece of Islamic art. He commissioned the creation of a new mihrab, a small but highly ornate room designed to *amplify* sound for prayer recitation. The mihrab was adorned with intricate mosaics made of gold and coloured glass, imported from Byzantium, reflecting a diplomatic alliance between the Umayyads and the Byzantine Empire. Al-Hakam II added a maqsura, an enclosure near the mihrab for the caliph and his entourage, further highlighting the mosque's political significance.

Al-Mansur extended the mosque's dimensions further to the east in the late 10th century and carried out the final major expansion. This structure could hold thousands of worshippers. The mosque became the largest in the Islamic West and a focal point for religious and intellectual life in Córdoba, one of the world's most advanced cities, by the 10th century.

The Great Mosque of Córdoba's architectural innovations include its double-tiered arches, which allowed for higher ceilings and a sense of grandeur, and its unique blending of styles. The courtyard (sahn), planted with orange trees, served as a serene gathering space for worshippers and scholars, emphasising the connection between nature and spirituality in Islamic architecture. The structure's emphasis on light, symmetry, and geometric precision reflected Islamic culture's spiritual and artistic ideals.

In 1236, after the Reconquista, Córdoba was captured by Christian forces led by King Ferdinand III of Castile, and the mosque was consecrated as a cathedral. Over the centuries, modifications were made to reflect its new function, including adding a Renaissance-style nave and bell tower in the 16th century, commissioned by Charles V, Holy Roman Emperor. Despite these changes, much of the mosque's original Islamic architecture remains intact, preserving its unique fusion of cultural influences. The Great Mosque of Córdoba is also a UNESCO World Heritage site!

We cannot conclude the Andalusian architecture of the Golden Age of Islam without talking about Alhambra. The Alhambra, located in Granada, Spain, is a breathtaking palace-fortress complex that epitomises the architectural and artistic achievements of the Nasrid dynasty during the final chapter of Islamic rule in Al-Andalus. Construction of the Alhambra began in 1238 CE under Muhammad I Ibn al-Ahmar, the founder of the Nasrid dynasty. It continued over a century, with significant additions by rulers such as Yusuf I (1333–1354 CE) and Muhammad V (1354–1391 CE). Built atop Sabika Hill overlooking the city, the Alhambra was conceived as a defensive fortress and a symbol of Nasrid's power, demonstrating the dynasty's sophistication amidst increasing political and military pressures from the advancing Christian Reconquista.

The Alhambra's name derives from the Arabic "Al-Qal'a al-Hamra", meaning "The Red Fortress," referring to the reddish hue of its walls made from local clay. Initially, Muhammad I fortified the site, adding towers and defensive walls to establish Granada as the Nasrid capital. The palace's transformation into an architectural masterpiece occurred during the reigns of Yusuf I and Muhammad V, who commissioned the construction of luxurious palaces, tranquil courtyards, and intricate gardens that reflected the cultural ideals of Islamic Spain. The Alhambra embodies the Moorish style, characterised by geometric precision, delicate arabesques, and an intimate connection with nature, making it one of Europe's finest examples of Islamic architecture.

The complex has three main sections: the Alcazaba (fortress), the Nasrid Palaces, and the Generalife Gardens. The Alcazaba, the oldest part of the Alhambra, served as a military stronghold. Its massive towers, such as the Torre de la Vela, provided panoramic views of Granada and the surrounding Sierra Nevada mountains. The Nasrid Palaces, however, are the crown jewels of the Alhambra, showcasing the dynasty's artistic and architectural brilliance. The Palacio de Comares (Court of the Myrtles) was the official residence of the sultan and a symbol of Nasrid's authority, featuring a tranquil reflecting pool surrounded by intricate stucco work and arched windows. The Hall of the Ambassadors, located within the Comares Palace, boasts a spectacular domed ceiling of cedar wood adorned with geometric patterns symbolising the cosmos. This hall was the throne room, where the sultan received dignitaries and conducted state affairs.

The Palacio de los Leones (Court of the Lions), constructed during Muhammad V's reign, is perhaps the most iconic section of the

Alhambra. The courtyard features a central fountain supported by 12 intricately carved marble lions, symbolising strength and sovereignty. Surrounding the courtyard are delicate arcades with slender columns and elaborate muqarnas (stalactite) carvings, creating an ethereal interplay of light and shadow. Adjacent to the Court of the Lions is the Hall of the Abencerrajes, with its radiant star-shaped dome, and the Hall of the Two Sisters, adorned with intricate tile mosaics and stucco reliefs. These spaces reflect the Nasrid emphasis on ornamentation, symmetry, and the integration of poetry and architecture; inscriptions in Arabic praise of Allah and extol the glory of the sultan.

The Generalife, the Alhambra's summer palace and gardens, is a serene retreat that exemplifies the Islamic ideal of paradise. Built in the 14th century, it features lush greenery, cascading water features, and carefully arranged terraces harmonising with the natural landscape. The Generalife served as a peaceful escape for the Nasrid rulers, offering respite from the demands of court life while reflecting their refined taste and spiritual connection to nature.

The construction and decoration of the Alhambra were carried out by skilled artisans and architects, many of whose names remain unknown. The intricate tilework, stucco carvings, and wooden ceilings showcase the expertise of Nasrid artisans, who combined local Andalusian techniques with influences from North Africa and the Islamic East. The inscriptions throughout the complex, written in Kufic and cursive scripts, were composed by court poets and served as decoration and spiritual reminders, with phrases such as "Wa la Ghalib illa Allah" (There is no victor but Allah) recurring prominently.

The fall of Granada in 1492 CE to the Catholic Monarchs Ferdinand and Isabella marked the end of Islamic rule in Spain. The Alhambra was converted into a royal palace, and subsequent alterations introduced Renaissance elements, such as the Palace of Charles V, an incongruous addition built in the 16th century. Despite these changes, much of the original Nasrid architecture remains intact, thanks to preservation efforts over the centuries. In the 19th century, the Romantic movement in Europe revived interest in the Alhambra, inspiring artists, writers, and historians, including Washington Irving, whose book "Tales of the Alhambra" brought the site global recognition. The Alhambra is also a UNESCO World Heritage Site!

Out of all the structures we discuss in this part, the next one is the most obscure, for reasons unknown, or should I say, the least famous, yet very significant. The Great Mosque of Samarra, located in Samarra, Iraq, is one of the most iconic architectural achievements of the Abbasid Caliphate. Built between 848 and 851 CE, it was commissioned by Caliph Al-Mutawakkil (r. 822–861 CE), one of the most influential rulers of the Abbasid dynasty. This mosque, once the largest in the world, reflected the Abbasids' ambition to showcase their empire's cultural and religious dominance. Located in the new capital of Samarra, which Al-Mutawakkil established to consolidate his authority and distance himself from political factions in Baghdad, the mosque became the centrepiece of the city's grand urban design.

The mosque was built under the direction of chief architect Al-Farghani, an astronomer and engineer of Persian origin who was also involved in scientific projects under the Abbasid court. Al-Farghani worked with a team of skilled artisans, masons, and labourers to create a functional structure that was a place of worship and symbolic of Abbasid power. The mosque's construction took approximately three years, a remarkable feat given its vast size and intricate design.

The Great Mosque of Samarra is renowned for its colossal dimensions, covering an area of 240,000 square meters. The rectangular plan, typical of early Islamic mosques, featured a spacious courtyard (sahn) surrounded by a collonaded prayer hall. The prayer hall, supported by 464 massive brick piers, could accommodate tens of thousands of worshippers, reflecting the Abbasids' desire to create a monumental space befitting their empire's capital. The mosque's walls were constructed from baked brick and adorned with stucco carvings featuring intricate geometric and vegetal patterns, showcasing the artistic refinement of the Abbasid period.

One of the mosque's most distinctive features is its spiral minaret, known as the Malwiya Minaret, which rises to 52 meters. The minaret is connected to the mosque by a 33-meter bridge, although this has not survived intact. The tower's unique design consists of an external spiral ramp that circles the structure seven times, allowing easy ascent to the top. The minaret served as a platform for the call to prayer (adhan) and a symbol of the Abbasid Caliphate's architectural innovation and grandeur. Its unusual form believed to have been inspired by Mesopotamian ziggurats, reflects the Abbasids' ability to integrate local influences into their architectural traditions.

The mosque's massive outer walls, measuring 10 meters in height, were punctuated by 44 semicircular buttresses, providing structural stability and an imposing visual effect. A grand gateway marked the main entrance on the northern side, further emphasising the mosque's monumental scale. The mosque's interior was relatively austere compared to its exterior, a characteristic of early Islamic architecture that prioritised space and functionality over elaborate decoration in the prayer area.

The Great Mosque of Samarra played a pivotal role in the religious and social life of the Abbasid capital. It was a centre for communal prayer and a hub for scholarly activity and public gatherings. The mosque's vast courtyard and colonnades provided spaces for education and discourse, reflecting the Abbasid commitment to fostering intellectual and spiritual growth.

Over the centuries, the mosque suffered significant damage due to neglect, invasions, and natural disasters. By the 13th century, after the decline of the Abbasid Caliphate, the mosque fell into disuse, and much of its structure was reduced to ruins. However, The Malwiya Minaret has remained largely intact as a solitary testament to the mosque's former magnificence. In recent years, the site has been the focus of archaeological and preservation efforts, though it has faced challenges, including damage during military conflicts in Iraq.

The Great Mosque of Samarra's architectural legacy extends beyond its original function. Its design influenced later Islamic architecture, particularly the construction of large congregational mosques worldwide. The Malwiya Minaret, with its striking spiral form, remains a unique feature in Islamic architectural history and a symbol of Abbasid ingenuity. The Great mosque of Samarra is also a UNESCO World Heritage site!

We shall move our attention from Al Andalusia to Egypt, for a mosque was built there that imparts knowledge to students from across the globe today. Students who crave profound Islamic knowledge prefer this place as their first choice. Of course, I am talking about Al Azhar University in Cairo, Egypt. It didn't start as a university but as a mosque; from the onset, though, emphasis was placed on imparting Islamic knowledge by making it a centre of education.

The Al-Azhar Mosque, located in the heart of Cairo, Egypt, is one of the most significant monuments of the Islamic world, renowned not only for its architectural beauty but also for its pivotal role in the development of Islamic education. Constructed between 970 and 972 CE, it was commissioned by Jawhar al-Siqilli, the military commander of the Fatimid Caliph Al-Mu'izz li-Din Allah, following the Fatimid conquest of Egypt. The mosque's construction marked the establishment of Cairo (then newly founded) as the capital of the Fatimid Caliphate and the spiritual centre of their Ismaili Shi'a Islamic doctrine.

In time, Al-Azhar evolved into a Sunni institution and became one of the world's oldest and most prestigious centres of Islamic learning.

The mosque was named Al-Azhar in honour of Fatimah al-Zahra, the daughter of the Prophet Muhammad and a revered figure in Shi'a Islam, reflecting the Fatimid dynasty's Ismaili Shi'a heritage. Jawhar al-Siqilli employed skilled architects and artisans to design a structure reflecting the Fatimids' religious and political aspirations. Though the names of the chief architects are not recorded, the mosque's design reflects the architectural traditions of North Africa and the Islamic Mediterranean, blending influences from earlier structures in Tunisia and Sicily, regions previously under Fatimid control.

The initial construction of the mosque featured a central courtyard (sahn) surrounded by three arcades and a modest prayer hall with five aisles. The mosque was relatively small in its original form, emphasising simplicity and functionality. The mihrab (prayer niche) and minbar (pulpit) were intricately decorated, setting a precedent for later embellishments. The minarets, added in later periods, became defining features of the mosque's skyline. The architecture of Al-Azhar reflects the early Fatimid style, characterised by harmonious proportions, clean geometric lines, and restrained ornamentation.

In 975 CE, it was established as a centre for teaching and scholarship, making it the first formal Islamic university. The mosque hosted classes on Quranic studies, jurisprudence (fiqh), theology, and the sciences, attracting scholars from across the Islamic world. By the 12th century, under the rule of Salah al-Din (Saladin), Egypt transitioned from Fatimid Shi'a rule to Sunni dominance. Al-Azhar shifted its focus to Sunni theology, becoming a bastion of Sunni Islamic thought.

Al-Azhar underwent numerous expansions and renovations, reflecting the architectural styles of successive dynasties, including the Ayyubids, Mamluks, Ottomans, and modern Egyptian rulers. The Ayyubids, under Salah al-Din, were the first to reconfigure the mosque for Sunni practices, adding classrooms and restoring the building's integrity. The Mamluks, known for their love of intricate decoration, significantly expanded Al-Azhar, adding three prominent minarets, which remain some of its most iconic features. These minarets were designed by master artisans such as Qanibay al-Rammah, showcasing intricate carvings, calligraphy, and arabesque patterns. The Ottomans, in turn, introduced domed structures and expanded the prayer hall to accommodate the growing number of worshippers and students.

One of Al-Azhar's most transformative periods was during the 19th and 20th centuries when the mosque became the focal point of Egypt's Islamic revival. Modernisation efforts included the introduction of electricity, new classrooms, and library facilities, ensuring the institution remained a relevant and dynamic centre of Islamic learning. Today, Al-Azhar University, which evolved from the mosque, offers courses in various subjects, including the sciences, humanities, and modern disciplines, while remaining firmly rooted in Islamic studies.

The architectural features of Al-Azhar reflect the layered history of its construction. The minarets, including the double-tiered minaret of Al-Ghuri and the Mamluk-era Qaytbay minaret, are among its most recognisable features, symbolising the mosque's status as a beacon of Islamic knowledge. The mosque's interior is adorned with elegant mashrabiya screens, stucco decorations, and Quranic inscriptions. The sahn, or courtyard, remains the heart of the mosque, surrounded by arcades supported by marble columns. As the intellectual hub of Islamic learning, it has shaped Islamic thought and jurisprudence for over a millennium. Scholars trained at Al-Azhar played pivotal roles in disseminating Islamic knowledge, standardising Sunni theology, and resisting colonial influences during the modern era. The mosque and university also served as centres for interfaith dialogue, reflecting the inclusive spirit of Islamic civilisation. Al Azhar is also a UNESCO World Heritage site! When monumental structures were built, Islamic architecture reached its zenith between 1400 and 1600. However, I argue that the Mughals built one of the finest to be built in India. It is called The Taj Mahal; though not a mosque or a knowledge-imparting institute, it stands tall as an epitome of love and Islamic achievements.

While the Mughals did not build the Taj Mahal during the Golden Age of Islam, it was influenced by earlier Islamic architecture. It is now the epitome of thousands of years of brilliance and meticulously designed architecture.

The Taj Mahal, built between 1632 and 1648 CE in Agra, India, is a crowning achievement of Mughal architecture and an enduring symbol of love.

Emperor Shah Jahan commissioned it as a mausoleum for his beloved wife, Mumtaz Mahal. The Taj Mahal reflects the synthesis of Persian, Islamic, and Indian architectural traditions, heavily influenced by earlier Islamic monuments, particularly those from the Golden Age of Islam.

The Taj Mahal derives much of its inspiration from Islamic architectural principles developed in earlier mosques and mausoleums. A centralised dome—a defining feature of Islamic architecture—is reminiscent of structures such as the Dome of the Rock and the Blue Mosque, emphasising symmetry and celestial symbolism. The four minarets surrounding the central dome echo the mosque layout, symbolising a sacred space. These minarets are slightly tilted outward to prevent collapse onto the main structure during an earthquake, showcasing advanced engineering knowledge.

The Taj Mahal's char bagh (four-part garden) layout is inspired by Persian garden design and symbolises paradise as described in the Quran. This garden concept was previously used in Alhambra's Generalife Gardens and other Islamic architectural masterpieces. The intricate calligraphy and geometric inlays on the Taj Mahal's white marble façade draw directly from the decorative traditions of earlier mosques, such as the Great Mosque of Córdoba and the Great

Mosque of Samarra. The Quranic inscriptions, crafted by the calligrapher Amanat Khan, further reinforce the Islamic heritage.

Additionally, the Taj Mahal's massive iwan (arched portal) and the interplay of light and shadow in its design mirror the grand entrances of mosques such as the Al-Azhar Mosque. The emphasis on reflection, seen in the water pools leading up to the structure, recalls the reflective courtyards of Islamic mosques, creating an ethereal connection between the earthly and the divine.

While the Taj Mahal is primarily a mausoleum, its architectural language is deeply rooted in Islamic traditions. It blends earlier mosque aesthetics with

Mughal innovations. The Taj Mahal is a timeless monument that demonstrates how the Mughal Empire borrowed and elevated the architectural heritage of the Islamic world to create one of humanity's greatest architectural wonders. Do I even need to highlight that it is also a UNESCO World Heritage site?

I have concluded with the same sentence for every structure I discussed throughout this section. It is not a coincidence that I chose to do that, nor is it that all these sites are recognised and protected by UNESCO as World Heritage Sites. They are testaments to the incredible achievements of our builders, architects, and patrons. It is a matter of concern that this needs to be highlighted, and many of us aren't aware of these accomplishments.

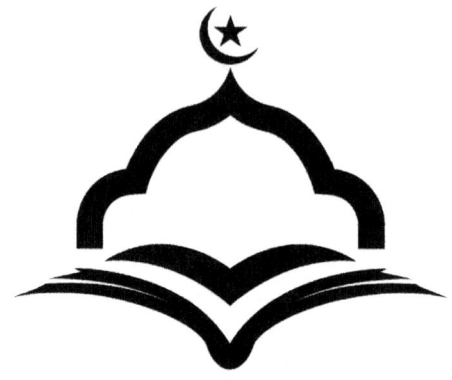

16

ISLAMIC CALLIGRAPHY ART

"Calligraphy is the geometry of the soul expressed through the body, a harmony that reflects the balance of creation itself."

– Ibn Muqla

Another example of Islamic art is Arabic calligraphy and Islamic art (Islamic Geometry and Illumination). Each of the monuments discussed above is extensively adorned by Arabic Calligraphy carvings and Islamic Geometric patterns that are not just complex but are equally intriguing and beautiful; the complexity stems from the fact that the designers delved more deeply into the intricate designs.

If you were to ask an artist who specialised in Islamic geometry, they would say it takes decades to replicate what they did with brick and mortar on paper, such was the calibre of the architects. Multiple designs often combine to form an even denser and more complex design. So, when you see any Islamic monument again and are intrigued by a random crisscross pattern, know that a certain level of science, mathematics, and execution was required to achieve it with precision.

In every civilisation, documenting what is being learned and keeping a record are crucial. Going back centuries, from the moment humanity learned to keep records, we often find ourselves making notes of our achievements; even this book, for that matter, is a form of note-making for future generations. With Islamic civilisation, though, it was even more significant, as unlike any other language, Arabic is considered a "Calligraphy-centric" language; it has many different kinds of scripts, each being a calligraphy script. In other words, as I always loved to say in my workshops, "In Arabic, you don't just write, you calligraph". Therefore, most of our notetaking was done in some form of calligraphy. Arabic calligraphy has such deep roots that even the Quran is written in "Naskh, " one of the most written Calligraphy scripts.

One of the oldest known scripts is Kufi Mushafiya, or primitive kufi, the first designated script in which the Quran was written. The most famous of all scripts is Thuluth (one-third), the go-to script for adorning Mosques' walls or creating wall art. I will note a few stalwarts of Arabic Calligraphy who redefined the art of Arabic Calligraphy by introducing the more proportioned and cursive calligraphy, an approach far from the primitive rectilinear elongated Kufic Script.

Ibn Muqla-Father of Arabic Calligraphy:

Abu Ali Muhammad ibn Ali ibn Muqla (885–940 CE) is celebrated as one of the most influential figures in the history of Arabic calligraphy, earning his place as the pioneer of the proportional script system that revolutionised Islamic art and ensured its enduring legacy. Born in Baghdad during the Abbasid Caliphate, Ibn Muqla's life was marked by his immense contributions to calligraphy, high-ranking political career, and tragic downfall. His innovations established the foundation for Arabic calligraphy's aesthetic and technical principles, and his work inspires calligraphers today.

Abbasid Caliphate commissioned Ibn Muqla to write the rules of a new form of Calligraphy writing, which would be smaller and easier to read and write, to make Mushaf (Qur'an) more petite in size and easier to carry and become portable. In the *Naskh* script, Ibn Muqlah introduced rounded forms and curved lines that, in later styles, were refined to give Arabic writing the flowing beauty for which it is renowned. Although *Naskh* was initially intended to copy the Qur'ān, by the 11th century, it was used widely for royal and everyday correspondence and as architectural decoration. This was a revolution; it was only after this that the size of the Mushaf was reduced, and they were being used widely. And proof of that is in your house…!(although Ibn Muqal didn't lead this revolution, his student did, as you will see shortly).

Ibn Muqla wrote the rules for six scripts: Naskh, Thuluth, Muhaqqaq, Raihani, Riqa', and Tawqi. Together, they are called Aqlam Al Sitta, which translates to "the six pens." Over the centuries, all the scripts mentioned above were refined by several calligraphers. However, we still use the same Nuqta system to measure the letters, which we call Meezan! Ibn Muqla introduced this. Many letters retain similar shapes with a lot of refinement. However, that would be visible to the keen and trained eye…! These scripts still use the Golden Ratio.

But was there a need to bring about a change or introduce these scripts at all? Yes, you see, the script used at the time to write the Qur'an was Kufi, specifically called Kufi Mushafiya, primitive Kufi, or primary Kufi, which is rectilinear and has much wider letters. This demanded huge parchments to write just one ayah; hence, the application was limited to writing a few ayah, a surah, etc. A few Mushaf were commissioned and written, but those belonged to a small section of the society. That is when the Abbasid Caliphate decided there was a need to do things differently, and their act led to smaller, more rounded scripts instead of rectilinear ones, which enabled more written content and a smaller form factor. I mean, the Mushaf you get in Madina—you know how small that is.

By the way, Mushaf is also handwritten in every release, which might come as a surprise; I will talk more about it in the last part of this section, where I make a concluding comment on Arabic Calligraphy and a legend. Ibn Muqla is called the father of Arabic Calligraphy, and rightly so. Ibn Muqla and his brothers are considered originators of Khat Al Mansoob, which means "The Proportionate Scripts" in simple words. These scripts have governing rules which define the measurements of every letter.

Ibn Muqla had many noteworthy students who advanced the scripts, refining them as they went along... The most well-known student of Ibn Muqla is Ibn Al-Bawwab, who gained a timeless reputation for mastering the script Ibn

Muqla used. Abū Hayyān al-Tawhīdī and Yaqut al-Musta'simi were his other noteworthy disciples.

Yaqut al-Musta'simi would take the level of Naskh to even higher heights with multiple refinements, so much so that his followers made his school of thought on Naskh, which was considered the yardstick against which the writings were judged; his school was followed by Persian and Ottoman calligraphers exclusively! More on Yaqut al-Musta'simi to follow.

The latest refinement came when Mehmet Izzah from Turkey introduced many significant changes, harmonised the shapes of letters, and brought Consistency to Naskh. Later, it became known as Ottoman Naskh, slightly different from Yaqut Al-Musta'simi. His students formed another school of thought on Naskh, and the Mushaf being written came to be known as Uthmani Mushaf. Yes, it is derived from the word Ottoman, not from Uthman (R.A), the fourth Caliph!

Ibn Muqla also held several positions in the Abbasid Caliphate. He was a Vazier and served three different terms as a Vazier. Due to many political disputes and civil wars, Ibn Muqla found himself on the other side of governance and was imprisoned for the latter part of his life. The military ruler at the time ordered his right hand and tongue to be cut off. He used the same hand with which he re-defined the rules of Arabic calligraphy, yet he kept writing with a prosthetic arm; such was his dedication.

Ibn Muqla died at the age of 54-55 in Baghdad in prison on 20th July 940. Ibn Muqla is a standout personality in the field of Arabic Calligraphy; it is thanks to him that you and I can write such beautiful scripts, and we owe him at least a small gratitude; his story is not told amongst calligraphers as vividly as it should be. I will end this story with a huge revelation: many of us think Arabic Calligraphy rules are written in Turkey, but that is not correct; many noteworthy calligraphers from Turkey have indeed led the sceptre of Arabic Calligraphy for centuries, and the contributions of the Ottomans is unparalleled, yet the fact remains, the rules were Refined in turkey, not **Defined**. They were done by Ibn Muqla in Baghdad under the patronage of the Abbasids.

Of the many who learned Arabic calligraphy from Ibn Muqla, one of the foremost is Ibn al Bawwab, whose name translates as Son of the Doorkeeper!

He was accomplished in law and theology, devout, and said to have recited the Qur'an from memory. Ibn Al Bawaab was also an accomplished painter, illuminator, and Calligrapher, a rare combination. He studied calligraphy with the Daughter of Ibn Muqla. He was fluent in all six scripts, which we discussed in the first episode of the artist profile: Aqlaam As shittah, which is Thuluth, Naskh, Muhaqqaq, Raihani, Riq'aa, and Tawqi.

Ibn Al Bawwab came to be known for his handwritten Quran, the likes of which had never been done before; while many of his works were destroyed by Mongol attacks, few survived. His work was copied and re-written by generations of calligraphers; most of his work was Qur'an-centric and brought the most significant change in the way the

Qur'an was approached, not just in being written but also in the way it was being read…! Hence, most of the points discussed here are about his contributions to making the Qur'an easily accessible and readable!

Ibn al-Bawwāb produced 64 copies of the Qur'an—six manuscripts with colophons identifying him as the calligrapher survived. The only surviving Qur'an bearing his name is the famed copy at the Chester Beatty Library in Dublin, Ireland.

Ibn al-Bawwāb was recognised as a master in his own time; his calligraphy school lasted until Baghdad fell to the Mongols more than two centuries after his death. One of his most outstanding achievements was the perfection of the al-Khatt al-Mansub (literally, *the well-proportioned script*).

Let me shed some light on the only surviving manuscript Ibn Al Bawwab wrote.

Chester Beatty Library Qur'an

Illuminated Headings for Chapters 108-113 from the Ibn al-Bawwab Qur'an. The sole surviving Qur'an penned by Ibn al-Bawwab, housed at the Chester Beatty Library, is the earliest example of a paper-based Qur'an manuscript. Representing a transition from Kufic or semi-Kufic Qur'ans transcribed on parchment or vellum, the Chester Beatty manuscript is written entirely in rounded, cursive script on paper. It contains 286 folios.

Additionally, the text is fully vocalised, with vowels and consonants written in the same colour ink. In short, "Fathah Kasrah Dammah" was also part of the text. Unlike its parchment and vellum predecessors, this paper Qur'an was oriented vertically rather than horizontally. Let me explain. When Kufi was used to writing the Quran, the books were horizontally oriented because Kufi is a rectilinear script. However, Ibn Al Bawwab changed that to vertical orientation.

Let me tell you what that means; pick your Qur'an and observe how it is oriented; you will notice that almost all Qur'ans are vertically oriented. It is a rectangular book with taller vertical sides and shorter horizontal sides. If I were to give you a context, the book was not oriented like a laptop screen in a horizontal orientation; instead, it was like an iPad in a vertical orientation. This was done by Ibn al Bawwab!

He even changed how calligraphers used spacing; allow me to cite an example. Previous calligraphers had used symmetrical spacing; Ibn al-Bawwab did it asymmetrically, extending one letter to create a large gap between words, drawing the reader's eyes across the page and demarcating a new section. You can now see this in the Basmallah we write in Thuluth and Naskh; the next time you read Basmallah, observe how the *kasa* of Seen stretches before it connects with the meem. That was done by Ibn Al Bawwab. Regarding the spacing of the verses, he left no spaces between individual verses, marking them with small, triangular clusters of blue dots instead.

However, every fifth and tenth verse includes spacing filled with the standard gold markers. For the first time, the leftward tilt was used to write; earlier scripts were either straight or had rightward tilt, like Hijazi script, which posed a unique challenge in continuity of reading, so he changed it to left tilt to encourage you subconsciously to continue to read, he would even use sublinear flourishes, which we call Kasheeda, to make the eye of the reader keep the continuity of reading, also making it easier to read... talk about he being a great Calligrapher, this even qualifies him as a psychologist who makes you think!

The quality of Ibn al Bawwab was so high that he rarely required underlined pencil work on which final work is generally done. Once he decided how to write, he would write it without any outlined sketch. In addition to writing the Qur'an, he was also a versatile artist; he could work with paint on the wall, on a large scale, and with Qalam on a small scale... As stated earlier, he was also an Illuminator and, most often, illuminated his Qur'an himself. His writings always stupefied the people around him. He would cut his qalam and never show anyone how; he would always do it out of everyone's sight...! His letters were not often identical; he would vary the letter shapes slightly, sometimes in the same line; in many ways, that showed he was a thinking man; however, the letters followed the rules of harmony, design and proportion.

His letters are not identical, but looking at the page gives the impression of even writing—quite a paradox! The page of Ibn Al Bawwabs's Qur'an measures 17.5 and 13.5 cm; in short, it is just the size of a small notebook and contains 15 lines. Let me give you a context: a standard display Qur'an, when staked one over the other, measured around 6 feet in height. Compare that to the book that could fit your pocket—now that is perspective! (second one in the book)

Every time you travel and carry a Quran, remember the name Ibn al Bawwab because he made it possible. By making the Quran smaller, many more people could read it privately, ensuring private piety rather than public display! Three critical aspects of Ibn Al Bawwab and his Qur'an and how they inspired generations are apparent even today!

• It was first ever written on paper, not on vellum, parchment, or papyrus.
• It was written in Naskh
• That it was small.

These points to a common desire: to make the Quran easily accessible to ordinary people in ordinary situations. It is known that, upon his death in 1022 CE, he was buried in Baghdad near the tomb of Ahmad Ibn-Hambal.

Before Ibn Al Bawwab, no single wholly written Qur'an existed in Naskh or anywhere else. After he wrote the first Qur'an in Naskh, dozens were copied and written; such was his impact.

Ibn al Bawwab is the reason why you have a small Quran today; Ibn Al Bawwab is the reason why the text in the Quran is legible today; he is the reason why your hands don't pain when you pick up and read the Quran for hours. He is why you can afford to buy a Quran; he is why you can connect with your Rabb privately!

Another big name that we should discuss is Yaqut Al Musta'simi. His journey is that of a classic enslaved person who rises to the upper echelons of success. Some records call him the Qibla of Arabic Calligraphy; we will soon know why.

Yaqut never really wrote the rules of any new script; on the contrary, he refined Naskh and Thuluth to many extents; his Naskh and Thuluth resemble the Naskh and Thuluth we write today. Yaqut al-Musta'simi was born during the 13th century, likely in Baghdad, the cultural and intellectual hub of the Abbasid

Caliphate. His name, al-Musta'simi, indicates that he was initially an enslaved person in the service of Caliph Al-Musta'sim, the last Abbasid caliph before the fall of Baghdad to the Mongols in 1258. Yaqut was emancipated by the caliph and, under his patronage, received a comprehensive education, which included training in theology, literature, and the arts.

Despite the turbulent political climate of the 13th century, marked by the Mongol invasions and the eventual destruction of Baghdad, Yaqut found solace in the refinement and practice of calligraphy. He turned his craft into a lifelong pursuit, achieving artistic heights that would immortalise his name in the annals of Islamic art. One of Yaqut's most significant contributions was his emphasis on penmanship. He advocated cutting the pen at an oblique angle rather than straight across to allow for greater control over the width and curvature of strokes. This technique gave his writing a sense of fluidity and elegance that became the hallmark of his style. The way to measure how significant this was is to express that from that day to this day, Arabic Calligraphy has never gone back to straight-cut reed pens (Qalams). And if you are an Arabic calligrapher, you owe the ease of writing with oblique cut qalam nib to Yaqut. Yaqut's precise and disciplined approach to penmanship became a model for subsequent generations of calligraphers. A keen eye could tell if the script was written by

Yaqut or some other calligrapher just by looking at his letter shapes, especially the shape of Waow, which is considered the most challenging letter in Naskh and Thuluth. Unlike Ibn Muqla, whose letters weren't identical but created overall harmony, Yaqut's letters were similar in shape (in principle), which was the hallmark of his writing.

Yaqut also strongly emphasised the interplay between negative space and the written word, ensuring that the layout of his compositions was as visually pleasing as the letters themselves. His work was characterised by its consistent adherence to the principles of harmony and proportion by carefully applying Ibn Muqla's proportional script system.

Yaqut al-Musta'simi was a prolific scribe who produced numerous Quranic manuscripts revered for their artistry and precision. His manuscripts are noted for their meticulous execution, with every letter and word carefully aligned to create a seamless text flow. These works often featured ornate Thuluth headings and Naskh body text, which became standard in Quranic calligraphy (practised to this day).

While the exact number of Qurans he produced is still being determined, surviving examples of his work are housed in prestigious collections, including the Topkapi Palace Museum in Istanbul and the British Library in London. These manuscripts exemplify his unparalleled skill and dedication to the art form, with intricate marginal decorations, delicate gold illuminations, and harmonious page layouts.

Yaqut's calligraphy extended beyond Quranic manuscripts, including architectural inscriptions and other decorative works. His style influenced the adornment of mosques, madrasahs, and other religious buildings, ensuring his artistic legacy was integrated into the Islamic world's built environment.

Post the Golden Age of Islam, Turkish calligraphers took up the sceptre of carrying the art on their shoulders and, to a large extent, did that single-handedly, with contributions from other areas. Ottoman Caliphs wanted to leave an indelible mark on the world, and they decided to do that with Arabic Calligraphy; they introduced scripts like Taliq, Diwani, and Diwani Jali. Diwani was notably developed during the reign of Mehmed the Conqueror in the 15th century; the purpose of this script was to write royal decrees (farmans), but later was adopted as an ornamental script, especially Diwani Jali.

Unlike other art forms, Arabic calligraphy continues to flourish even today, though it is limited to geographies like Turkey, Iran, Iraq, and Egypt, which are the major contributors.

As promised at the beginning of the chapter, here is the process followed while producing our Mushaf (Qur'an). First, Ustadh Uthman Taha, based in Madina, writes the Qur'an manually, with qalam. That is then digitised, checked for corrections, and sent for printing. The print you see, if it is the Uthamani Qur'an, is first handwritten every time a new edition comes out. This was a revelation to me, and I thought I would share it with you as a concluding remark for the chapter.

We now shift our focus to the Americas; you might ask, what do Muslims have to do with the Americas? Buckle up, or be prepared to jump off your seats!

17

CHRISTOPHER COLUMBUS FOUND AMERICAS...REALLY?

"The scientific achievements of the Islamic Golden Age laid the foundations for the Age of Discovery. Tools like the astrolabe, navigational charts, and advances in cartography—perfected by Muslim scholars—allowed European explorers to venture further and chart new worlds."

– Jim Al Khalili

Social science is another area where Islamic scholars from the Golden Age of Islam flourished, from making the most accurate map of the world at the time to carefully concluding the presence of a landmass to the far west, in other words, discovering the Americas! Yes, controversially, I will make my point that Muslims were one of the foremost who discovered America and not Christopher Columbus.

Although it is a fundamental point of debate, what do we even mean by "Discovering Americas"? Americas always existed; people lived there, communicated with their contemporaries, and exchanged culture and ideas, as we will see shortly. I don't intend to offend the people who always lived there and called it their home; I only wish to speak in a common language that we all associate with humankind, realising that the world's boundaries didn't end at the farthest point of Africa in the west. So, if any native Indians happen to read this book, I apologise in advance if any of this offends you. With that, let me bust the story of how "Christopher Columbus discovered America." And I request you to trust me when I say that the end of this will tie in with the book's topic, The Golden Age of Islam; I only request that you read it thoroughly.

An old saying goes, "Until the lion learns to write, every story will glorify the hunter." Long have we lived and heard the stories from the hunter. Our schools taught us that Christopher Columbus was on a fantastic voyage to find India and "accidentally" discovered America, and I will present one proof that shows otherwise. Around 889 CE, A geographer named Al Masudi wrote about a journey from the port of Delba that lasted for months and reached a landmass. His accounts state that they traded with locals and returned home. Delba is the same port from which Christopher Columbus set sail in 1492. Is that a coincidence?

A map includes an "unknown land" across the Atlantic Ocean. Note they used to have inverted maps with the South at the top and the North at the bottom. How could a geographer from 889 know about a landmass without prior knowledge? Mainly because the Atlantic Ocean was described as an Ocean of darkness. If I oversimplify this achievement with an example, it is like you saying there is grass on the other side of a mile-long tunnel without ever entering it. This was no coincidence.

Al Idrees also wrote about the same, stating sailors travelled for 31 days, reached a land mass and were taken captive but later released.

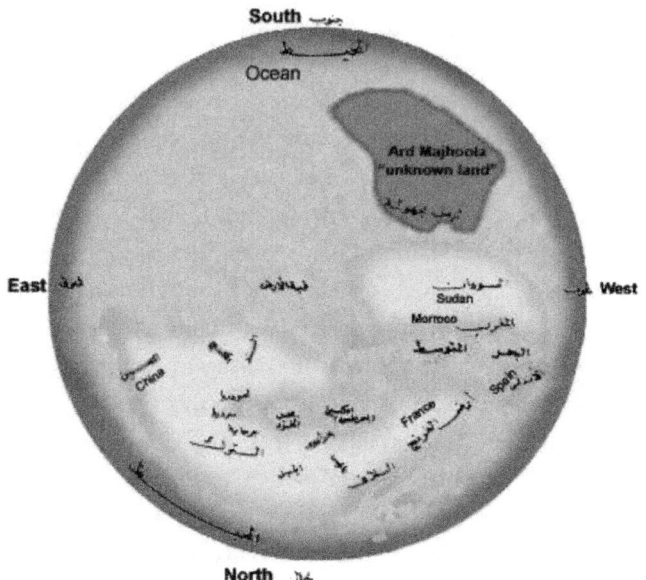

While one can scoff this off by stating this is inconclusive, one cannot decline the fact that Vikings had contact with the Americas (now Canada) and set up their colonies hundreds of years before Christopher Columbus; either way, the conclusion holds that there was contact with Americas long before Columbus discovered Americas. This, coupled with Al Masudi's talk about "an Unknown land", raises many questions. These will take much time to substantiate (if one honestly wants to), yet they are facts one should know! This brings me to the greatest cartographer of the 9th century, Al Idrisi!

Al-Idrisi's most significant contributions came during his time at the court of King Roger II of Sicily, a Norman ruler who sincerely appreciated Islamic knowledge. Roger II ruled over a multicultural kingdom where Muslims, Christians, and Jews coexisted, creating an atmosphere of intellectual exchange. Recognising Al-Idrisi's expertise, Roger invited him to Palermo in 1138 CE to create a comprehensive geographical compendium and a world map.

Under Roger's patronage, Al-Idrisi worked for nearly two decades, drawing on his travels, knowledge of classical texts, and reports from travellers and merchants. His project culminated in creating the Tabula Rogeriana (The Book of Roger), one of the most advanced and detailed works of geography and cartography.

Tabula Rogeriana was Completed in 1154 CE; the Tabula Rogeriana was a comprehensive atlas of the known world, accompanied by a detailed text titled "Nuzhat al-Mushtaq fi Ikhtiraq al-Afaq" ("The Pleasure of Him Who Longs to Cross the Horizons"). Following Islamic cartographic tradition, the map depicted the world as a circular disk, with the south at the top and the north at the bottom. It covered regions from the Atlantic to the Indian Ocean, including Europe, Africa, and Asia. It also detailed descriptions of over 70 major cities, mountain ranges, rivers, and trade routes.

The Tabula Rogeriana remained one of the most accurate maps of the medieval period, influencing European cartography well into the Renaissance. Its precision in representing distances, coastlines, and topographical features reflected Al-Idrisi's commitment to empirical observation and mathematical accuracy.

Al-Idrisi is credited with creating a large silver disc world map for King Roger II. This map, reportedly engraved with detailed geographic information, measured approximately 3.5 meters in diameter. Although the silver disc has been lost to history, it is widely regarded as a remarkable achievement of medieval engineering and cartography.

Al-Idrisi's geographical texts detailed various regions' economies, cultures, and societies. For example, he provided insights into the silk trade in China, gold production in Africa, and maritime trade in the Indian Ocean.

His work documented the medieval world's interconnectedness, emphasising the importance of trade routes and exchanging goods and ideas.

Al-Idrisi's maps featured detailed coastlines, rivers, and mountain ranges, emphasising accuracy and practical utility for travellers and merchants. His maps used grid lines and mathematical principles to depict spatial relationships, a precursor to modern cartographic techniques.

The Tabula Rogeriana has survived the tumultuous times and is still preserved in various libraries worldwide; the most critical copy is at Bibliothèque Nationale de France (National Library of France). Bodleian Library. Oxford University holds a manuscript copy of Al-Idrisi's Nuzhat al-Mushtaq fi Ikhtiraq al-Afaq. Vatican Library and Topkapi are other museums/libraries with records of his work.

From Al Idrisi's most detailed map to the educated deduction of "an unknown land" based on his calculations, Geographers from the Golden Age of Islam practically mapped the whole world for the Europeans, only for them to use these maps and go on the "Discovery of the world". And yet you and I have never heard about these incredible figures, either because they were overshadowed or their work was not credited to the correct "name" as the names were Latinized; it lost its connection to their heritage. Today, even though we gave Europe most of the knowledge they garnered, we stand primarily unrecognised. And Yet we gave it to the Europeans. Graciously!

18

WE GAVE IT TO THE EUROPEANS.
GRACIOUSLY!

"For five centuries, from 700 to 1200, Islam led the world in power, order, and extent of government, in refinement of manners, scholarship, science, medicine, and philosophy."

– Will Durant

If you have reached here, I will make a bold statement: this part of the book is arguably the most important; let me make my point and explain what I mean by that. You have read through the book (hopefully enjoyed it and learnt significantly till now), and you now know who the stalwarts were; it is now the time to understand how their work was transferred to other civilisations and, therefore, if their work exists, and if so, through which translator, in which book, so should you come across that book, your mind should start knocking, reminding you of who was the original writer of the concepts discussed in that book.

We have been cut off from our legacy because we came across facts, learnt it is from the Europeans, and stopped; we didn't look further because it didn't sound familiar. I blame the Latinisation of names; while it was done for ease of pronunciation, I believe it later manifested into something more cynical, to hide the legacy of Muslims from us. Would you instead connect your Muslim roots to Algorithmi or Al Khwarizmi? Avicenna or Ibn Sina? Hopefully, you get the point. With that said, let us look at the complete translation movement in detail.

You will notice that my tone here is a bit appreciative of the movement, as I acknowledge that we had our translation movement and made further advancements in respective fields. As a writer, I must bring forth all points in front of you so you are well-equipped with knowledge from both ends of the spectrum. As I have said in the forthcoming pages, if it were up to the academics, scientists, and scholars, we would still have great Islamic names much higher up with the greatest of the greats in human history.

The translation movement from Arabic to Latin, spanning the 11th to 13th centuries, was one of medieval history's most transformative intellectual endeavours. It marked a pivotal period when Europe rediscovered the knowledge of antiquity and the groundbreaking contributions of Islamic scholars through translations of Arabic texts into Latin. This intellectual exchange bridged the Islamic and European worlds and laid the *foundation* for the European Renaissance. The movement was concentrated in cultural and academic hubs such as Toledo, Sicily, and Southern Italy, where the convergence of Christian, Muslim, and Jewish scholars facilitated the transmission of knowledge. These translations covered various disciplines, including philosophy, medicine, astronomy, mathematics, and natural sciences.

The origins of this movement can be traced back to the early Islamic world, which had already experienced its own Translation Movement during the Abbasid Caliphate (8th–10th centuries). The Abbasids had translated Greek,

Roman, Persian, and Indian texts into Arabic, fostering a golden age of scientific and philosophical inquiry. Pioneering figures like Al-Kindi, Al-Farabi, and Hunayn ibn Ishaq synthesised and expanded upon the works of Aristotle, Ptolemy, Hippocrates, and others. By the time this knowledge was transmitted to Europe, it represented the classical heritage of antiquity and the innovations of Islamic scholars.

The translation movement into Latin gained momentum during the Reconquista of Spain and the Norman conquests of Sicily, where territories with significant Muslim populations fell under Christian rule. These regions became the epicentres of intellectual exchange. Toledo, in particular, emerged as a vital hub. After the city was recaptured by Christian forces in 1085 CE, it retained its rich Islamic and Jewish intellectual traditions. The Cathedral of Toledo, under the patronage of Archbishop Raymond of Toledo, became a key institution for translations. Christian, Jewish, and Muslim scholars worked together, often using Arabic as a linguistic bridge to translate texts into Latin.

One of the most influential figures in this movement was Gerard of Cremona (1114–1187 CE), an Italian scholar who travelled to Toledo to access the vast libraries of Arabic texts. Gerard translated over 70 significant works, including Ibn Sina's Canon of Medicine and Ibn al Haytam's Book of Optics. These texts introduced Europeans to advanced astronomical theories, sophisticated medical practices, and the principles of optics and light. Gerard's translations were instrumental in shaping the curricula of medieval European universities.

Another prominent figure was Adelard of Bath (1080–1152 CE), an English scholar who travelled extensively in the Islamic world, including Spain, Sicily, and possibly the Levant. Adelard was particularly interested in mathematics and astronomy. He translated Arabic astronomical texts and introduced concepts like the astrolabe (a significant Muslim advancement), revolutionising navigation and celestial observation.

Under the rule of the Norman kings, particularly Roger II, another translation movement flourished in Sicily. The court of Palermo became a centre of cultural exchange, where scholars of various faiths collaborated. The most notable translator from this period was Michael Scot (1175–1232 CE), who worked on Arabic commentaries on Aristotle, including those by Ibn Rushd. (Averroes) Scot's translations were pivotal in transmitting Aristotelian philosophy to Europe, laying the groundwork for Scholasticism, a dominant intellectual tradition of medieval Europe.

Meanwhile, in southern Italy, scholars like Constantine the African (1017–1087 CE) played a crucial role in translating Arabic medical texts into Latin. Constantine, a North African who converted to Christianity and became a monk in Monte Cassino, translated numerous works, including Arabic pharmacological texts. These translations provided the basis for medieval European medicine and were studied at institutions like the Salerno School of Medicine.

Astronomy and mathematics were other fields in which Arabic translations profoundly impacted. Arabic texts introduced Europe to the Arabic numerals, which originated in India, along with the notation of zero (note: Notation of Zero and Concept of Zero are two separate things) and advanced algorithms. Translators like Adelard of Bath and Gerard of Cremona championed these innovations, revolutionising European mathematics. Similarly, works like Al-Zarqali's astronomical tables and Al-Battani's astronomical treatises, Al Tusi's couple, provided Europeans with more accurate models of celestial motion, eventually influencing the work of Copernicus.

Scholars like William of Moerbeke (1215–1286 CE) translated Arabic texts into Latin and mathematical treatises in France. William's efforts ensured that Arabic knowledge permeated the intellectual centres of northern Europe.

While the translation movement greatly enriched European intellectual life, it was not a one-way exchange. European scholars often expanded upon or adapted the Arabic texts they translated. For example, medieval European medicine and science were profoundly shaped by Arabic medical texts such as Ibn Sina's "Canon", which remained a standard reference in European universities well into the 17th century, blending Islamic, classical, and European knowledge, laying the foundation for the Scientific Revolution.

The translation movement also served as a bridge between cultures, fostering a spirit of intellectual curiosity and cooperation. Although it was partly driven by the era's political and religious conflicts, the collaboration of Christian, Muslim, and Jewish scholars demonstrated the universality of knowledge. It also highlighted the interconnectedness of human civilisations, as ideas from ancient

Greece and Rome were preserved and transformed in the Islamic world before being transmitted back to Europe.

By the 13th century, the translation movement began to wane. However, its impact endured as the knowledge translated from Arabic formed the foundation of medieval European education. Institutions like the University of Paris and the University of Bologna incorporated Arabic-translated texts into their curricula, ensuring their influence on generations of scholars.

While we must appreciate the work of the translators and other European scholars who advanced the groundbreaking works of Ibn Sina, Al Biruni, and Ibn

Al Haytham, we should also take it with a pinch of salt that we were then categorically discredited (or at least kept out of the public domain).

As I said in the introduction of this chapter, while Latinisation may have started with an innocuous notion of spreading knowledge, it took a cynical path of masking the achievements of Muslims from The Golden Age of Islam. The academic community is above the petty thoughts of political influence, and religious affinity plays little to no role in the collaboration; one cannot deny that the real power vests in the hands of those who call themselves kings, rulers, and ministers, for those are the ones who dictate what goes out in schools, colleges and universities and what remains masked and hidden. Ever wonder why the great library of the Vatican is sealed to the common public? I'd like to know what gems are kept away from our knowledge and how the world would change should they be made public. These are the answers perhaps we will never get in our lifetime; nevertheless, like I said a few times in the book, and I will repeat it here, we need to start connecting with our ancestral achievements, our history just like every civilisation clings on its historical successes to show what a great civilisation it is!

The best way is to know who the writers and the translators were and what the books are named today, so if you happen to see the book in your academic circle, you would know. And with that intention in mind, I am listing below. Names of the books, their writers, their translators, and the book's name by when it is known today!

1. Kitab al-Shifa (The Book of Healing)
   • Author: Ibn Sina (Avicenna)
   • Latinized Name: Avicenna
   • Translator: Gerard of Cremona
   • City/Country: Toledo, Spain
   • Modern Title: *The Book of Healing* (Philosophical Encyclopedia)
2. Al-Qanun fi al-Tibb (The Canon of Medicine)
   • Author: Ibn Sina (Avicenna)
   • Latinized Name: Avicenna
   • Translator: Gerard of Cremona
   • City/Country: Toledo, Spain
   • Modern Title: *The Canon of Medicine* (Medical Canon)
3. Kitab al-Manazir (Book of Optics)
   • Author: Ibn al-Haytham (Alhazen)
   • Latinized Name: Alhazen
   • Translator: Gerard of Cremona
   • City/Country: Toledo, Spain
   • Modern Title: *The Optics of Alhazen*
4. Al-Zij al-Sabi (The Sabian Tables)
   • Author: Al-Battani (Albatenius)
   • Latinized Name: Albatenius

- Translator: Plato of Tivoli
- City/Country: Barcelona, Spain
- Modern Title: *The Sabian Tables* (Astronomical Tables)

5. Tahafut al-Tahafut (The Incoherence of the Incoherence)
   - Author: Averroes (Ibn Rushd)
   - Latinized Name: Averroes
   - Translator: Michael Scot
   - City/Country: Toledo, Spain
   - Modern Title: *The Incoherence of the Incoherence*

6. Kitab al-Jabr wa al-Muqabala (The Book of Algebra)
   - Author: Al-Khwarizmi (Algoritmi)
   - Latinized Name: Algoritmi
   - Translator: Robert of Chester
   - City/Country: Segovia, Spain
   - Modern Title: *The Book of Algebra* (Foundational Algebraic Text)

7. Kitab al-Tafsir (Commentary on Aristotle's Physics)
   - Author: Averroes (Ibn Rushd)
   - Latinized Name: Averroes
   - Translator: Michael Scot
   - City/Country: Toledo, Spain
   - Modern Title: *Commentary on Aristotle's Physics*

8. Kitab al-Adwiya al-Mufrada (The Book of Simple Drugs)
   - Author: Al-Razi (Rhazes)
   - Latinized Name: Rhazes
   - Translator: Gerard of Cremona
   - City/Country: Toledo, Spain
   - Modern Title: *The Book of Simple Drugs* (Materia Medica)

9. Kitab al-Hawi (The Comprehensive Book on Medicine)
   - Author: Al-Razi (Rhazes)
   - Latinized Name: Rhazes
   - Translator: Gerard of Cremona
   - City/Country: Toledo, Spain
   - Modern Title: *The Liber Continens* (Comprehensive Medical Text)

10. Risala fi Istikhraj al-Mu'addalat (Treatise on Equations)
    - Author: Omar Khayyam
    - Latinized Name: Omar Khayyam
    - Translator: John of Seville
    - City/Country: Toledo, Spain
    - Modern Title: *Treatise on Algebraic Solutions*
11. Kitab al-Arba'in (Forty Hadiths)
    - Author: Al-Ghazali (Algazel)
    - Latinized Name: Algazel
    - Translator: Dominicus Gundissalinus
    - City/Country: Toledo, Spain
    - Modern Title: *The Forty Principles* (Theological Work)
12. Kitab al-Musiqa al-Kabir (The Great Book of Music)
    - Author: Al-Farabi (Alfarabius)
    - Latinized Name: Alfarabius
    - Translator: Gerard of Cremona
    - City/Country: Toledo, Spain
    - Modern Title: *The Great Book of Music*
13. Kitab al-Kimia (The Book of Alchemy)
    - Author: Jabir ibn Hayyan (Geber)
    - Latinized Name: Geber
    - Translator: Robert of Chester
    - City/Country: Segovia, Spain
    - Modern Title: *The Book of Alchemy*
14. Kitab al-Istiksar (Book of Reflections)
    - Author: Alhazen (Ibn al-Haytham)
    - Latinized Name: Alhazen
    - Translator: Gerard of Cremona
    - City/Country: Toledo, Spain
    - Modern Title: *The Book of Reflections* (Optics)
15. Kitab al-Athar al-Baqiya (Chronology of Ancient Nations)
    - Author: Al-Biruni
    - Latinized Name: Aliboron
    - Translator: Adelard of Bath

- City/Country: Sicily
- Modern Title: *Chronology of Ancient Nations*

16. Kitab al-Filaha (The Book of Agriculture)
    - Author: Ibn Bassal
    - Latinized Name: Bassalus
    - Translator: John of Seville
    - City/Country: Toledo, Spain
    - Modern Title: *The Book of Agriculture*

17. Kitab al-Asrar (Book of Secrets)
    - Author: Jabir ibn Hayyan (Geber)
    - Latinized Name: Geber
    - Translator: Plato of Tivoli
    - City/Country: Spain
    - Modern Title: *The Book of Secrets*

18. Kitab Rujjar (The Book of Roger)
    - Author: Al-Idrisi
    - Latinized Name: Dreses or Edrisi
    - Translator: Commissioned in Latin by Roger II (translated directly under Al-Idrisi's supervision)
    - City/Country: Palermo, Sicily
    - Modern Title: *The Tabula Rogeriana*

19. Al-Masalik wa al-Mamalik (The Routes and Kingdoms)
    - Author: Ibn Khordadbeh
    - Latinized Name: Ibn Cordoba
    - Translator: Unknown, transmitted through Arabic collections in Al-Andalus
    - City/Country: Toledo, Spain
    - Modern Title: *The Routes and Kingdoms*

20. Kitab al-Buldan (The Book of Lands)
    - Author: Al-Yaqubi
    - Latinized Name: Al-Yacubi
    - Translator: Parts translated by Adelard of Bath
    - City/Country: Spain or Sicily
    - Modern Title: *The Book of Lands*

21. Kitab al-Athar al-Baqiya (Chronology of Ancient Nations)
    - Author: Al-Biruni
    - Latinized Name: Aliboron
    - Translator: Adelard of Bath
    - City/Country: Spain or Sicily
    - Modern Title: *The Remaining Signs of Past Centuries*
22. Tarikh al-Rusul wa al-Muluk (History of the Prophets and Kings)
    - Author: Al-Tabari
    - Latinized Name: Al-Tabari
    - Translator: Partial translations by Herman of Carinthia
    - City/Country: Toledo, Spain
    - Modern Title: *The History of the Prophets and Kings*
23. Kitab al-Ibar (The Book of Lessons)
    - Author: Ibn Khaldun
    - Latinized Name: Ibn Khaldun
    - Translator: Translations initiated in the 16th century, following earlier partial translations of his work in Spain
    - City/Country: Spain and Renaissance Italy
    - Modern Title: *The Muqaddimah* (Prologue to Universal History)
24. Kitab al-Tarikh (Book of History)
    - Author: Al-Masudi
    - Latinized Name: Al-Masudi
    - Translator: Partial translations by scholars in Toledo
    - City/Country: Toledo, Spain
    - Modern Title: *Meadows of Gold and Mines of Gems*
25. Kitab al-Nafs (Book on the Soul)
    - Author: Avicenna (Ibn Sina)
    - Latinized Name: Avicenna
    - Translator: Michael Scot
    - City/Country: Toledo, Spain
    - Modern Title: *De Anima*
26. Kitab al-Siyasah (Book of Politics)
    - Author: Al-Farabi (Alfarabius)
    - Latinized Name: Alfarabius

- Translator: Gerard of Cremona
- City/Country: Toledo, Spain
- Modern Title: *The Book of Politics*

27. Kitab al-Najat (The Book of Deliverance)
- Author: Avicenna (Ibn Sina)
- Latinized Name: Avicenna
- Translator: Latin versions known through Toledo
- Modern Title: *The Book of Deliverance*

This list is by no means exhaustive and is only trying to be a starting point of a more profound journey should you be willing to undertake and learn about our ancestors. Everything that has a beginning has to have an end; that is the law of nature, as was the case with The Golden Age of Islam; however, unlike many who think it disappeared overnight in thin air, several factors led to the decline, and it took centuries for the age to decline. You will find my tone to be harsh here, especially towards our Muslim brothers and sisters, as I believe we have not done justice to our legacy and preserved our achievements. You might have to take this with a pinch of salt.

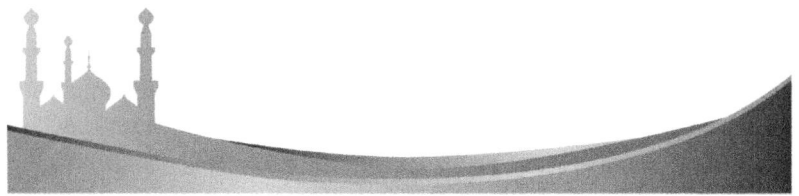

19

IT DIDN'T HAPPEN OVERNIGHT

"From a civilisation of questioners to blinder followers, we lost our Golden Age."

– Salim Khan

The decline of intellectual vibrancy in the Islamic world is a multifaceted issue rooted in historical, cultural, and political shifts. One of the most significant factors was the gradual retreat from scientific and philosophical inquiry, often influenced by theological pressures and socio-political instability. By the 12th and 13th centuries, the Islamic world began shifting its intellectual priorities from exploring natural sciences and philosophy to a more narrow focus on religious orthodoxy.

The rise of Ash'arism, a theological school that emphasised divine will over human reasoning (diving will is unquestioned, but abandoning human reasoning should be questioned), contributed to this intellectual shift. While early Islamic philosophers like Al-Kindi, Ibn Sina, and Ibn Rushd championed the use of reason and logic in understanding the natural world, later scholars viewed these pursuits with suspicion. Through works like *The Incoherence of the Philosophers*, figures such as Al-Ghazali critiqued and undermined the rationalist traditions of thinkers like Ibn Sina and Al-Farabi, labelling philosophy as a potential threat to Islamic theology. Although Al-Ghazali himself was a great intellect and contributed significantly to Islamic thought, his critique of philosophy discouraged future scholars from pursuing natural sciences with the same vigour.

This theological conservatism, combined with a growing focus on taqlid (imitation) rather than ijtihad (independent reasoning), created an intellectual climate in which innovation was stifled. Scholars began to focus on preserving and interpreting existing knowledge rather than advancing it, leading to stagnation in once-thriving fields like medicine, astronomy, and mathematics.

One of the most critical aspects of the decline was the Islamic world's gradual disconnection from its intellectual legacy. While Europe actively embraced and built upon the knowledge transmitted through translations of Arabic works, the Islamic world failed to preserve its pioneering spirit of inquiry.

While European scholars like Copernicus, Galileo, and Newton revolutionised science, the Islamic world had primarily abandoned its leadership role in these fields.

For instance, while Ibn al-Haytham's groundbreaking work on optics laid the foundation for modern physics, few Muslim scholars revisited or expanded his theories in later centuries. Similarly, Al-Khwarizmi's revolutionary algebraic methods and Ibn Sina's medical treatises remained static, studied more as historical artefacts than starting points for further innovation. Though advancements were made, they were more evolutionary than revolutionary.

This disconnect was exacerbated by colonial narratives that framed Islamic contributions as secondary to European achievements, further eroding confidence in the Islamic intellectual tradition. Even today, there is often a need for more awareness within the Islamic world about the profound impact of Golden Age scholars, perpetuating a cycle of undervaluing scientific and intellectual pursuits. The final nail in the coffin was the inability to adopt the printing press; while Europe openly embraced the approach of printing their books, the Islamic world chose not to; as a result, Europeans were able to produce work at a much faster rate and hence were able to spread the word quicker than Islamic scholars could, which resulted in Europeans reaching younger generations faster, more effectively, and by the time Islamic knowledge reached the same group of people they had already read about it earlier, and that is how the original knowledge became secondary. It is easier to write than express just how detrimental it proved for the knowledge to disseminate amongst the people; not embracing the printing press was us digging our graves!

Of course, other factors contributed to the decline; as I said earlier, it was a steady decline rather than an overnight disaster. One such factor that gravely affected the growth was the destruction of Baghdad by the Mongols.

The Mongol invasions of the 13th century dealt a devastating blow to the Islamic intellectual infrastructure. The sack of Baghdad in 1258 CE, often seen as a symbolic end to the Golden Age, destroyed the House of Wisdom and countless libraries, manuscripts, and scientific instruments. Baghdad, the intellectual heart of the Islamic world, had been a centre of translation, scholarship, and innovation. Its loss not only decimated the physical resources needed for intellectual pursuits but also shattered the morale of the Islamic world.

Although other learning centres, such as Cairo, Isfahan, and Samarqand, emerged to some extent, they could not replicate the same interconnected, multidisciplinary intellectual activity that characterised the Abbasid period. The Mongol invasions disrupted trade routes and communication networks, further isolating scholars and limiting the exchange of ideas. This, coupled with the fact that the Islamic world had been divided into several factions, contributed to this.

This political fragmentation of the Islamic world following the decline of the Abbasid Caliphate also contributed to intellectual stagnation. The once-unified Islamic empire fragmented into competing dynasties, such as the Seljuks, Mamluks, and Ottomans, each with its priorities and challenges. While some rulers continued patronising scholars, the scale of intellectual investment paled compared to the Golden Age. Many rulers focused on military expansion and consolidation of power, leaving little room for fostering centres of learning.

By contrast, Europe, emerging from its own Dark Ages, began investing heavily in universities and scientific research during the Renaissance, spurred by the knowledge it inherited from the Islamic world. European rulers and merchants provided steady funding to scholars, enabling the development of modern scientific methods. The Islamic world, in turn, failed to institutionalise its scientific achievements, which remained confined mainly to individual scholars or court-sponsored projects.

Despite the broader narrative of intellectual stagnation, there were pockets of continuity where scientific and cultural pursuits persisted. The Ottoman Empire, for instance, maintained some level of scientific activity through institutions such as the Istanbul Observatory, established by Taqi al-Din in the 16th century. Similarly, the Mughal Empire in India fostered advancements in architecture, medicine, and astronomy, blending Islamic traditions with local knowledge.

However, these efforts were often isolated and needed the systemic, collaborative approach that characterised the Golden Age. The absence of a unified intellectual vision meant that, though significant, these achievements needed to be revised to counteract the broader trend of stagnation.

Arguably, the Golden Age of Islam began with "a grain of doubt," which led to the monumental work of Ibn Al Haytham and other scientists (to this day); the decline began when we stopped doubting and started taking things at face value just because our Shaikh said so! Interestingly, this approach is only for "our Shaikhs" and not for the other faction of the Madhab (Maslak); we openly doubt every word from them. Now that I have laid my thoughts bare, let me also give you a point to be proud of.

The Golden Age of Islam was one of the most extended and influential periods in the medieval world. Let me cite an example to prove my point: the age of the USA is barely 200 years old, and many are already of the opinion that it is past its prime and is on the path to decline. The UK, which occupied half the world, lasted barely 300 years. The Golden Age of Islam lasted 500 years. That is no small feat. Mainly because the medieval world was a place of constant conflicts and conquests, and for any intellectual progress to be achieved, the prerequisite is *Peace*. Islamic Caliphate had achieved it for over 800 years of existence. This is only possible with the inclusion, collaboration, and appreciation of great minds. For example, the scholars were paid their weight in gold for their achievements. They valued knowledge; this contrasts with how we treat our teachers. An Imam in a masjid earns barely enough to get by; we openly champion that the Quran should be taught for free and yet complain about the lack of good-quality teachers. Here, I exclude those who cannot afford it genuinely and criticise those who can pay but don't see the value in spending as the Quran should be taught for FREE! You don't have to agree with me, but look around you; every institute has flourished because patrons value knowledge. However, not all is lost; it is heartening to see Islamic nations investing in scientific research and development and keeping consistent with their religious values. Today, we have started to speak about the Quran and Science in a single sentence again (I am sure it was the case during The Golden Age of Islam). Many of our Shaikhs now bring up points on how science is proving such and such. In contrast, the Quran said it 1400 years ago, while the objective here is not to show that science is advancing but to prove the authenticity of the Quran, which in itself shows the state of our inability to spread the word of the Quran effectively, to begin with.

We have been cut off from our history, ancestral achievements, and legacy for a long time. Several reasons exist, from Mongol invasions to burning 400,000 manuscripts from the Library of Cordoba. From Christian conquests and decimation of knowledge to the civil war between different sects of Islam, we ought to take the blame upon ourselves. It is not too far-fetched to say that we Muslims dug our graves. Centuries later, our generation is facing intellectual oppression; we are constantly challenged to prove our knowledge and looked down upon as a civilisation that has given nothing to this world except suicide bombers and men with masks carrying guns terrorising people. Cornered and left dumbfounded, we have no substantial response to those allegations. But that can change; "You" can be that change, and it is ironic as nothing aforementioned would have come to pass if we followed the first command of the Quran, "Iqra", meaning Read!

NOT A GOODBYE BUT JUST A START

Thank you for reading the entire book. I repeat: I am no writer and have no history of writing books. I am a mere mortal who seeks knowledge. I tried to bring back a few glimmers of hope to our current and future generations. However, I cannot do it alone. I am only one man trying my best.

I want to give you an idea of how difficult it was to dream about this, let alone write it and make it reach your hands. By the way, this is a boring story, so you can skip it; however, if you intend to read it down to the last word, I will ask you a big favour. If you are ready…read along.

I reverted to Islam about 7 years ago, though I was born in a Muslim family, which was not a practising family, and I was an agnostic! I always asked questions about everything, while what I saw around me was a group of blind followers, which was never my cup of tea. Therefore, I stayed away. But something happened 7 years ago that opened my eyes to how our Prophet (pbuh) lived his life and set a benchmark in front of me. I remember a saying by someone that goes, "Islam is the best religion but has the worst followers" While I don't wholly agree with it, I did see glimpses of that. Yet the same person also said, "Be the change you want to see," and so I did.

After accepting Islam, I made one Du'a; I didn't want to read the translation of the Quran; I wanted to know the Quran the way it is, in Arabic, and the almighty opened the doors for me. Fast forward to a pivotal moment in my life, with all that is happening with Muslims in my country and around the world, I had a "grain of doubt" about the way we are being demonised; it cannot be that we have not contributed anything to this world except you know what! And so, I started digging. My wife was a bit anxious, as she knew if I put my mind to something, I would get zoned out; I cut myself off and dedicate myself to the task. And I did such a thing. I owe an apology to her, my mother, and my daughter.

I began by reading incredible books like "The House of Wisdom- How Arabic Science Saved Ancient Knowledge and Gave Us the Renaissance" by Jim Al Khalili. What an apt title, I might add. I got many other books I immersed myself in and was surrounded by these books (I am old school). As detailed as these books are, it was not enough. I wanted more, so I started researching research papers and scholarly journals. What I came across was astonishing, from the names of the stars to the star charts themselves, from the first automata to the entire irrigation system, from the most detailed map of the world to predicting the presence of land in the far West (Americas), everything has Islamic influence written all over it. They tried very hard to cover it up or make alterations; however, it was all there to be read for the keen eye, and it still is. This is when I started posting videos on Instagram about all my learnings, hoping that I would get a lot of appreciation for it, and I did...!

However, I also got a lot of abuse, unprecedented, and I was left wondering, **why?** What did I say in this video that offended people so much? To my surprise, all these haters were not Muslims, and it all started to make sense (although I still believe they are only a minority). However, their nasty comments and messages propelled me to take this giant leap and write this book. I didn't know how long I would keep making videos and what would happen if the inevitable happened (The page shuts down, the account is blocked, or worse, I die). I wanted this legacy to live on. And so I began!

Besides research, I cut myself off from Instagram, Facebook, and YouTube. I sat down with my learnings and began writing. I didn't think about how to secure a publishing company, whom to approach with the book, who prints it, etc...

I spent over 3 months conceptualising and writing the book (I am sure there are many mistakes) and intend to spend many months or years spreading the book among the masses. After having worked tirelessly, I was able to secure a publishing company White Falcon Publishing, to whom I owe honest gratitude. I faced a lot of apparent hurdles; they didn't bother me, and they only pushed me to go further and dig deeper. I had no access to the libraries around Europe that hold multiple manuscripts of the books written by these giants (Yes, we still have many manuscripts preserved). I had no access to funding, which enabled me to travel to places I have referred to in the book; everything you read here has been written in my tiny room where I work. Everything you read is written in a simple Word document on my laptop. At every stage of writing the book, I double-guessed my work, corrected my writing, and re-wrote the entire chapter often to be more articulate and easy to read and follow; I am not sure if I did a good job at it, but I will let you be the judge.

However, this book is not the end of the road; it is just the beginning of a bright path I have embarked on; as I said in the preface, I have only scratched the surface. While there are books available on the market already, no writer has dedicated his life to this era, and I could not find multiple books written on the topic by a single person, so I intend to do so. I have already decided what my next book will be and my following four books. However, it is impossible without you, and this is where I ask for that favour I discussed at the beginning of this: "NOT A GOODBYE, BUT JUST A START."

Together, we stand firm. Together, we can defeat the narrative that Muslims are destructive and unproductive. I want you to spread the word. Once you have finished reading it, hand over this copy to your friend, or better yet, ask your friend to purchase it. That way, I will get your support, earn a small amount, and keep my endeavour ongoing for decades (Hopefully).

Share it on social media, and do not ignore the power you have at your hands; the more you share and encourage others to buy the book, the more you will spread the word of our ancestral achievement, the more our current generation and the next generation will connect with our accomplishments. We could see the next Ibn Al Haytam or Ibn Sina from our next generation. But it all starts with you, right now, in this moment with "A grain of thought".

ESSENTIAL INFORMATIONAL GLOSSARY OF SCHOLARS FROM THE GOLDEN AGE OF ISLAM:

- Abbas Ibn Firnas (810–887): An Andalusian polymath who made one of the earliest recorded attempts at human flight using a glider. He also designed innovative water clocks and contributed to astronomy and mechanics.
- Abu al-Barakat al-Baghdadi (1080–1165): A philosopher and physician who critiqued Aristotelian metaphysics and proposed ideas on motion that prefigured Newtonian concepts.
- Abu al-Qasim al-Zahrawi (Albucasis) (936–1013): Known as the "Father of Modern Surgery," he authored *Kitab al-Tasrif*, detailing over 200 surgical instruments and methods still relevant today.
- Abu Ma'shar al-Balkhi (Albumasar) (787–886) was a Persian astronomer synthesising Greek and Indian astronomical traditions. His works influenced medieval European astrology.
- Abu Nasr Mansur (970–1036) was a mathematician who specialised in spherical geometry. His contributions were foundational to trigonometry and astronomy.
- Abu Rayhan al-Biruni (973–1048): A prolific polymath who accurately measured the Earth's circumference and authored comparative religion, astronomy, and geography studies.
- Abu Yusuf Yaqub al-Kindi (Alkindus) (801–873): Often called the "Philosopher of the Arabs," he made significant advances in cryptography, optics, and the philosophy of science.
- Ahmad ibn Tulun (835–884): An architect and military leader who founded the city of Al-Qata'i and built the iconic Ibn Tulun Mosque in Cairo.
- Al-Asma'i (740–828) was a philologist and zoologist who was one of the earliest contributors to Arabic natural science and linguistics.
- Al-Ash'ari (874–936): A theologian and founder of Ash'arism, which became a dominant school of Islamic theology, harmonising reason with revelation.

- Al-Battani (Albatenius) (858–929): An astronomer who refined Ptolemy's planetary models and produced highly accurate astronomical tables that influenced Copernicus.
- Al-Farabi (Alfarabius) (872–950): After Aristotle, he was known as the "Second Teacher." He made groundbreaking contributions to metaphysics, ethics, political philosophy, and music theory.
- Al-Khwarizmi (780–850): A mathematician who wrote foundational texts on algebra, introducing algorithms and influencing Islamic and European mathematics.
- Al-Razi (Rhazes) (854–925) was a Persian physician and chemist. His works, including *Al-Hawi*, were significant sources of medical knowledge in medieval Europe.
- Al-Zahrawi (Albucasis) (936–1013): A surgeon whose innovations in medical practice and surgical tools shaped the field of medicine for centuries.
- Banu Musa Brothers (9th century): Three brothers who wrote *The Book of Ingenious Devices*, describing 100 mechanical inventions, including automata.
- Bar Hebraeus (1226–1286): A Syriac scholar who excelled in medicine, philosophy, and history, bridging Islamic and Christian intellectual traditions.
- Chaghmini (Mahmud ibn Muhammad al-Chaghmini) (13th century) was an astronomer whose textbook on Ptolemaic astronomy became widely studied in the Islamic world and Europe.
- Dawud al-Antaki (16th century): A physician and pharmacist who compiled medical knowledge into *Tadhkirat Uli al-Albab*, an encyclopedia of diseases and treatments.
- Fariduddin Attar (1145–1221): A Sufi poet best known for *The Conference of the Birds*, a metaphorical exploration of spiritual enlightenment.
- Fakhr al-Din al-Razi (1149–1209): A theologian and philosopher who wrote on cosmology, medicine, and metaphysics, emphasising the use of reason in understanding faith.

- Haly Abbas (930–994): A Persian physician whose *The Complete Book of the Medical Art* was a precursor to Avicenna's *Canon of Medicine*.
- Hassan al-Rammah (13th century): An engineer who documented early uses of gunpowder and designed military devices, such as torpedoes.
- Hunayn ibn Ishaq (Johannitius) (809–873): A translator and physician who brought Greek medical and philosophical texts into Arabic.
- Ibn Abi Usaybi'a (1203–1270): A historian of medicine who documented the contributions of Islamic and pre-Islamic physicians in *The History of Physicians*.
- Ibn al-Baitar (1197–1248): A botanist and pharmacologist who compiled *The Book of Simple Drugs*, cataloguing over 1,400 medicinal plants.
- Ibn al-Haytham (Alhazen) (965–1040): Known as the "Father of Optics," he made revolutionary discoveries about vision, light, and scientific methodology.
- Ibn al-Nafis (1213–1288): A physician who discovered the pulmonary circulation of blood, challenging Galenic theories.
- Ibn Battuta (1304–1369) was a Moroccan explorer whose travelogue provided invaluable insights into the Islamic world and beyond during the 14th century.
- Ibn Firnas (810–887): An inventor and engineer who attempted human flight and designed early mechanical devices.
- Ibn Khaldun (1332–1406) was a historian and sociologist. His *Muqaddimah* is considered the first work on history and social science philosophy.
- Ibn Sina (Avicenna) (980–1037): A polymath and physician whose *Canon of Medicine* was the definitive medical textbook for centuries.
- Ibn Zuhr (Avenzoar) (1091–1161): A surgeon and pharmacologist who significantly contributed to clinical medicine and pharmacology.
- Jabir ibn Hayyan (Geber) (721–815): Known as the "Father of Chemistry," he introduced experimental methods to alchemy and chemistry.

- Jalal al-Din Rumi (1207–1273): A Sufi poet and mystic; his works, including *Masnavi-i Ma'navi*, explore themes of divine love and human spirituality.
- Kamal al-Din al-Farisi (1267–1319): A physicist and mathematician, he explained the phenomenon of rainbows using geometrical optics.
- Lubna of Cordoba (10th century): A mathematician and librarian who worked in Andalusia's royal library, contributing to scholarship in mathematics and astronomy.
- Mahmud al-Kashgari (1005–1102) was a linguist and geographer who authored the *Compendium of the Turkic Dialects*, a foundational work on Turkic languages.
- Mansur ibn Ilyas (14th century) was an anatomist who produced one of the earliest anatomical atlases, including circulatory system diagrams.
- Maryam al-Asturlabi (10th century): An astronomer and astrolabe maker whose instruments were critical for navigation and timekeeping.
- Muhammad al-Tusi (Nasir al-Din Tusi) (1201–1274): A mathematician and astronomer who developed the Tusi Couple, a geometric model that influenced later Copernican theories.
- Nur al-Din al-Bitruji (Alpetragius) (12th century): An astronomer who proposed an alternative planetary system based on uniform circular motion.
- Qutb al-Din al-Shirazi (1236–1311): A polymath who expanded on Ibn al-Haytham's optical theories and contributed to astronomy and medicine.
- Rashid al-Din Hamadani (1247–1318): A historian and physician who compiled *Jami' al-Tawarikh*, a comprehensive world history.
- Rufayda al-Aslamiyya (7th century) is often considered the first Muslim nurse. She pioneered medical care and training during the Prophet Muhammad (PBUH).
- Sabur ibn Sahl (d. 869): A pharmacist who wrote *Aqrabadhin*, the first known formulary for preparing and prescribing medicines.
- Sharaf al-Din al-Tusi (1135–1213): A mathematician who solved cubic equations using geometric methods, paving the way for algebraic development.

- Sibawayh (760–796) was a linguist and grammarian. His *Al-Kitab* is the foundational text of Arabic grammar.
- Taqi al-Din (1526–1585): An Ottoman scientist who built an advanced observatory and developed clocks with mechanical innovations.
- Uqba ibn Nafi (622–683): A military leader and city planner who founded Kairouan, Tunisia's significant cultural and religious centre.
- Zayn al-Din al-Jurjani (1040–1136): A physician whose *The Treasure of the Khwarazm Shah* was a comprehensive medical reference.
- Ziryab (78F9–857): A musician and cultural innovator who revolutionised Andalusian music, cuisine, and fashion.
- Al-Dinawari (815–896): A botanist and astronomer whose *Kitab al-Nabat* is one of the earliest comprehensive studies of plants.
- Al-Taftazani (1322–1390): A theologian and logician who wrote extensively on Islamic philosophy and linguistics.
- Al-Fazari (Ibrahim ibn Habib) (8th century): An astronomer and mathematician credited with constructing the first astrolabe in the Islamic world.
- Ibn al-Shatir (1304–1375): An astronomer whose planetary models anticipated aspects of the Copernican system.
- Ibn Qutaybah (828–889): A historian and philologist who compiled one of the earliest Arabic encyclopedias, covering many topics.
- Al-Mas'udi (896–956): A historian and geographer who wrote *Meadows of Gold*, an influential work combining history, geography, and cultural insights.
- Thabit ibn Qurra (826–901): A mathematician and astronomer who contributed to statistics and developed theories in geometry.
- Fatima al-Fihri (9th century): The founder of Al-Qarawiyyin University in Fez, Morocco, the world's oldest continuously operating university.

BIBLIOGRAPHY

- Kennedy, Hugh. The Prophet and the Age of the Caliphates: The Islamic Near East from the 6th to the 11th Century. Routledge, 2016.

- Gutas, Dimitri. Greek Thought, Arabic Culture: The Graeco-Arabic Translation Movement in Baghdad and Early Abbasid Society (2nd-4th/8th-10th centuries). Routledge, 2000.

- Al-Khalili, Jim. The House of Wisdom: How Arabic Science Saved Ancient Knowledge and Gave Us the Renaissance. Penguin Books, 2011.

- Nasr, Seyyed Hossein. Science and Civilization in Islam. Harvard University Press, 1968.

- Ahmed, Leila. Women and Gender in Islam: Historical Roots of a Modern Debate. Yale University Press, 1992.

- Hillenbrand, Carole. Islam: A New Historical Introduction. Thames & Hudson, 2015.

- Sarton, George. Introduction to the History of Science. Carnegie Institution of Washington, 1927.

- Saliba, George. Islamic Science and the Making of the European Renaissance. MIT Press, 2007.

- Hourani, Albert. A History of the Arab Peoples. Harvard University Press, 1991.

- Berkey, Jonathan P. The Formation of Islam: Religion and Society in the Near East, 600–1800. Cambridge University Press, 2003.

- Ahmed, S. (2017). The Golden Age of Islam and its Impact on Modern Science

- Al-Khalili, J. (2012). Pathfinders: The Golden Age of Arabic Science. London: Penguin Books.

- Nasr, S. H. (2007). Science and Civilization in Islam. Cambridge, MA: Harvard University Press.

- Gutas, D. (2001). Greek Thought, Arabic Culture: The Graeco-Arabic Translation Movement in Baghdad and Early Abbasid Society. London: Routledge

- Hillenbrand, C. (2005). Islam: A New Historical Introduction. Edinburgh: Edinburgh University Press

- Kennedy, H. (2004). The Prophet and the Age of the Caliphates: The Islamic Near East from the Sixth to the Eleventh Century.

- Rosenthal, F. (1975). Knowledge Triumphant: The Concept of Knowledge in Medieval Islam.

- Makdisi, G. (1981). The Rise of Colleges: Institutions of Learning in Islam and the West. Edinburgh: Edinburgh University Press.

- Ehsan, M. (2019). The House of Wisdom: How Arabic Science Saved Ancient Knowledge and Gave Us the Renaissance. New York: Viking Press

Bibliography

- Rashed, R. (1994). The Development of Arabic Mathematics: Between Arithmetic and Algebra. Dordrecht: Springer.

- Sabra, A. I. (2007). "The Appropriation and Subsequent Naturalization of Greek Science in Medieval Islam: A Preliminary Statement." History of Science, 25(2), 223–243.

- Adamson, P. (2016). Philosophy in the Islamic World: A History of Philosophy Without Any Gaps. Oxford: Oxford University Press.

- Kraemer, J. L. (1992). Humanism in the Renaissance of Islam: The Cultural Revival During the Buyid Age. Leiden: Brill.

- Gutas, Dimitri. Greek Thought, Arabic Culture: The Graeco-Arabic Translation Movement in Baghdad and Early 'Abbasid Society (2nd–4th/8th–10th centuries). Routledge, 2001

- Al-Ghazali. The Alchemy of Happiness. Translated by Claud Field, Islamic Texts Society, 1997.

- Nasr, Seyyed Hossein. Science and Civilization in Islam. Harvard University Press, 1968.

- Ibn Rushd (Averroes). The Decisive Treatise. Translated by Charles Butterworth, Brigham Young University Press, 2001.

- Al-Farabi. The Virtuous City. Translated by Richard Walzer, Clarendon Press, 1985.

- Rosenthal, Franz. Knowledge Triumphant: The Concept of Knowledge in Medieval Islam. Brill Academic Publishers, 2007.

- Fakhry, Majid. A History of Islamic Philosophy. Columbia University Press, 2004.

- Ibn Sina (Avicenna). The Metaphysics of Healing. Translated by Michael Marmura, Brigham Young University Press, 2005.

- Kennedy, Hugh. When Baghdad Ruled the Muslim World: The Rise and Fall of Islam's Greatest Dynasty. Da Capo Press, 2005

- Hodgson, Marshall G. S. The Venture of Islam: Conscience and History in a World Civilization, Volume 2: The Expansion of Islam in the Middle Periods. University of Chicago Press, 1974

- Al-Khalili, Jim. The House of Wisdom: How Arabic Science Saved Ancient Knowledge and Gave Us the Renaissance. Penguin Press, 2011

- Nasr, Seyyed Hossein. Science and Civilization in Islam. Harvard University Press, 1968

- Gutas, Dimitri. Greek Thought, Arabic Culture: The Graeco-Arabic Translation Movement in Baghdad and Early 'Abbasid Society (2nd–4th/8th–10th centuries). Routledge, 2001

- Kennedy, Hugh. When Baghdad Ruled the Muslim World: The Rise and Fall of Islam's Greatest Dynasty. Da Capo Press, 2005

- Rashed, Roshdi. Mathematics and Physical Sciences in the Islamic World. Encyclopedia of the History of Science, 2001

- Rosenthal, Franz. Knowledge Triumphant: The Concept of Knowledge in Medieval Islam. Brill Academic Publishers, 2007

- Makdisi, George. The Rise of Colleges: Institutions of Learning in Islam and the West. Edinburgh University Press, 1981.

- Sabra, Abdelhamid I. The Optics of Ibn al-Haytham. University of Chicago Press, 1989

- Ibn al-Nadim. Al-Fihrist. Translated by Bayard Dodge, Columbia University Press, 1970

- Turner, Howard R. Science in Medieval Islam: An Illustrated Introduction. University of Texas Press, 1997

- Hillenbrand, Carole. Islam: A New Historical Introduction. Thames & Hudson, 2015

- Ibn Sina (Avicenna). The Canon of Medicine. Translated by Gerard of Cremona, Kazi Publications, 2007

- Nasr, Seyyed Hossein. Science and Civilization in Islam. Harvard University Press, 1968

- Gutas, Dimitri. Greek Thought, Arabic Culture: The Graeco-Arabic Translation Movement in Baghdad and Early 'Abbasid Society (2nd–4th/8th–10th centuries). Routledge, 2001

- Turner, Howard R. Science in Medieval Islam: An Illustrated Introduction. University of Texas Press, 1997.

- Rosenthal, Franz. Knowledge Triumphant: The Concept of Knowledge in Medieval Islam. Brill Academic Publishers, 2007

- Al-Razi (Rhazes). Kitab al-Hawi (The Comprehensive Book on Medicine). Translated by Gerard of Cremona, National Library of Medicine Archives, 1970

- Hillenbrand, Carole. Islam: A New Historical Introduction. Thames & Hudson, 2015

- Makdisi, George. The Rise of Colleges: Institutions of Learning in Islam and the West. Edinburgh University Press, 1981.

- Sabra, Abdelhamid I. The Optics of Ibn al-Haytham. University of Chicago Press, 1989.

- Al-Zahrawi (Albucasis). Kitab al-Tasrif (The Method of Medicine). Translated by Gerard of Cremona, Library of Congress, 1985.

- Lane, Edward William. An Arabic-English Lexicon. Williams & Norgate, 1863

- Ibn Zuhr (Avenzoar). Kitab al-Taysir fi al-Mudawat wa al-Tadbir (The Book of Simplification Concerning Therapeutics and Diet). Translated by Gerard of Cremona, National Library of Medicine, 1980

- Kennedy, Hugh. When Baghdad Ruled the Muslim World: The Rise and Fall of Islam's Greatest Dynasty. Da Capo Press, 2005

- Rashed, Roshdi. Mathematics and Physical Sciences in the Islamic World. Encyclopedia of the History of Science, 2001

- Hujjat al-Mulk, Kitab al-Hawi fi al-Tibb (The Comprehensive Book of Medicine)

- Al-Razi, Kitab al-Mansuri fi al-Tibb (The Book of Medicine Dedicated to al-Mansur)

- Gerald of Cremona (Translator), Liber Almansoris

- Al-Razi, Kitab al-Judari wa al-Hasbah (Treatise on Smallpox and Measles)

- Vivian Nutton, Ancient Medicine

Bibliography

- Syed Nomanul Haq, Names, Natures, and Things: The Alchemist Jābir ibn Ḥayyān and His Oeuvre
- Y. Tzvi Langermann, Al-Razi's Medical Ethics and its Influence
- George Sarton, Introduction to the History of Science.
- Peter E. Pormann and Emilie Savage-Smith, Medieval Islamic Medicine
  - Z. Iskandar, A Catalogue of Arabic Manuscripts on Medicine and Science
- Katz, Victor J. A History of Mathematics: An Introduction. Addison-Wesley, 1998
- Kennedy, E. S. The Life and Work of Al-Biruni. Saqi Books, 2004
- Al-Khalili, Jim. The House of Wisdom: How Arabic Science Saved Ancient Knowledge and Gave Us the Renaissance. Penguin Press, 2011
- Nasr, Seyyed Hossein. Science and Civilization in Islam. Harvard University Press, 1968.
- Hogendijk, Jan P., and Sabra, Abdelhamid I. The Enterprise of Science in Islam: New Perspectives. MIT Press, 2003
- Toomer, G. J. Eastern Wisedome and Learning: The Study of Arabic in Seventeenth-Century England. Oxford University Press, 1996
- Rashed, Roshdi. Mathematics and Physical Sciences in the Islamic World. Encyclopedia of the History of Science, 2001
- Gutas, Dimitri. Greek Thought, Arabic Culture. Routledge, 2001
- Saliba, George. Islamic Science and the Making of the European Renaissance. MIT Press, 2007
- Ibn al-Haytham. The Optics of Ibn al-Haytham. University of Chicago Press, 1989
- Sarton, George. Introduction to the History of Science. Carnegie Institution of Washington, 1927
- Jim Al-Khalili. Science and Islam (BBC Documentary). BBC, 2009
- Gutas, Dimitri. Greek Thought, Arabic Culture: The Graeco-Arabic Translation Movement in Baghdad and Early Abbasid Society. Routledge, 2001
- Sabra, Abdelhamid I. The Optics of Ibn al-Haytham: Books I-III, On Direct Vision. University of Chicago Press, 1989
- Nasr, Seyyed Hossein. Science and Civilization in Islam. Harvard University Press, 1968
- Lindberg, David C. Theories of Vision from Al-Kindi to Kepler. University of Chicago Press, 1976
- Smith, Mark A. From Sight to Light: The Passage from Ancient to Modern Optics. University of Chicago Press, 2015
- Al-Khalili, Jim. Pathfinders: The Golden Age of Arabic Science. Penguin, 2010
- Rashed, Roshdi. The Development of Arabic Mathematics: Between Arithmetic and Algebra. Springer, 1994
- Hassan, Ahmad Y. Islamic Technology: An Illustrated History. Cambridge University Press, 1986.

- Turner, Howard R. Science in Medieval Islam: An Illustrated Introduction. University of Texas Press, 1997
- Hillenbrand, Carole. Islam: A New Historical Introduction. Thames & Hudson, 2015
- Nallino, Carlo Alfonso. Opus Astronomicum Alhazenis. 1914
- Sarton, George. Introduction to the History of Science. Carnegie Institution of Washington, 1927
- Kennedy, E. S. Studies in the Islamic Exact Sciences. American University of Beirut, 1983
- Ibn al-Haytham. Kitab al-Manazir (The Book of Optics). Translated by A.I. Sabra, Brigham Young University Press, 2001 experiments on light and vision.
- Al-Jazari. The Book of Knowledge of Ingenious Mechanical Devices. Translated by Donald R. Hill, Springer, 1974
- Journal by: Abdelghani Tbakhi(Department of Pathology and Laboratory Medicine, Hôtel-Dieu Grace Hospital, University of Western Ontario, Windsor, Ontario, Canada), Samir S. Amr(Pathology Services Division, Dhahran Health Center, Saudi Aramco Medical Services Organization, Dhahran, Saudi Arabia)
  - https://doi.org/10.5144/0256-4947.2007.464
- Holmyard, Eric J. Alchemy. Dover Publications, 1990
- Kraus, Paul. Jabir ibn Hayyan: Contribution à l'histoire des idées scientifiques dans l'Islam. Institut Français de Damas, 1942
- Nasr, Seyyed Hossein. Science and Civilization in Islam. Harvard University Press, 1968
- Levey, Martin. Arabic Alchemy and the Occult Sciences. Variorum Reprints, 1973
- Hill, Donald R. The Book of Knowledge of Ingenious Mechanical Devices by Al-Jazari. Springer, 1974
- Al-Khalili, Jim. Pathfinders: The Golden Age of Arabic Science. Penguin, 2010
- Newman, William R. Atoms and Alchemy: Chymistry and the Experimental Origins of the Scientific Revolution. University of Chicago Press, 2006
- Hassan, Ahmad Y. Islamic Technology: An Illustrated History. Cambridge University Press, 1986.
- Riddle, John M. Quid Pro Quo: Studies in the History of Drugs. Variorum, 1992
- Weisser, Ursula. Jabir Ibn Hayyan: A Great Chemist or a Pseudo-Scientist? Ambix, 1960
- Bailey, Harold. Science in Medieval Islam: An Illustrated Introduction. University of Texas Press, 1997
- Abu-Lughod, Janet L. Before European Hegemony: The World System A.D. 1250–1350. Oxford University Press, 1989.
- Dinawari, Ahmad Ibn Dawud Al-. Kitab al-Nabat (The Book of Plants). Translated and edited by Lothar Kopf, 1957
- Elgood, Cyril. A Medical History of Persia and the Eastern Caliphate. Cambridge University Press, 1951

- Sarton, George. Introduction to the History of Science. Carnegie Institution of Washington, 1927.

- Qays ibn al-Mulawwah (7th Century Arabia)

  Significance: Known as "Majnun" for his tragic love story with Laila, his poetry became the foundation for one of the most retold tales in Arabic, Persian, and Indian cultures.

  The tale of "Laila and Majnun" remains a cultural symbol of unrequited love and inspired poets such as Nizami Ganjavi and Amir Khusrau.

- Nizami Ganjavi (1141–1209 CE)

  o Works: Kamsa (Five Poems), including "Laila and Majnun."

  o Significance: His poetic version of "Laila and Majnun" added depth and character development, transforming the story into an epic. His work bridged Persian and Arabic literary traditions.

- Al-Mutanabbi (915–965 CE)

  o Works: Famous Qasida "If You See the Lion's Canines."

  o Significance: Revered as one of the greatest Arabic poets, Al-Mutanabbi's themes of ambition, bravery, and human frailty made his works timeless. His poetry also reflects the socio-political climate of the Abbasid Caliphate.

- Jalal al-Din Rumi (1207–1273 CE)

  o Works: Masnavi-i Ma'navi (The Spiritual Couplets), Divan-e Shams-e Tabrizi.

  o Significance: Rumi's mystical poetry on love, unity, and spiritual growth transcended cultural boundaries, inspiring readers worldwide. Lines such as "What you seek is seeking you" resonate universally.

- The Dome of the Rock (691–692 CE, Jerusalem)

  o Architectural Style: Byzantine and early Islamic.

  o Significance: The first Islamic architectural masterpiece, built under Caliph Abd al-Malik, symbolized Islam's theological and political ascendancy. Its inscriptions emphasize the unity of God and the finality of Muhammad's prophethood.

- The Great Mosque of Córdoba (784 CE, Spain)

- Architectural Innovations: Double-tiered arches, Byzantine mosaics.

- Significance: A symbol of the Umayyad dynasty's cultural and religious identity in Al-Andalus, it highlights the fusion of Roman, Visigothic, and Islamic architectural elements.

- The Alhambra (1238 CE, Granada, Spain)

- Key Features: Court of the Lions, Hall of the Ambassadors, Generalife Gardens.

- Significance: The pinnacle of Nasrid architecture, showcasing intricate stucco work, poetic inscriptions, and geometric precision, reflecting the sophistication of Islamic Spain.

- The Great Mosque of Samarra (848–851 CE, Iraq)

- Architectural Style: Abbasid.

- Significance: Once the largest mosque in the world, it introduced the spiral Malwiya Minaret, blending Mesopotamian ziggurat influences with Islamic architectural innovation.
- Al-Azhar Mosque (970–972 CE, Cairo, Egypt)
- Significance: Transitioned from a Shi'a Fatimid mosque to a Sunni university, becoming a global hub for Islamic knowledge. It remains an architectural and intellectual beacon.
- Taj Mahal (1632–1648 CE, Agra, India)
- Architectural Style: Persian, Islamic, and Indian synthesis.
- Significance: Symbolizes Mughal innovation and Islamic architectural principles, particularly symmetry, reflecting pools, and Quranic inscriptions.
- Ibn Muqla (885–940 CE)
- Contributions: Proportional script system (Aqlam al-Sitta).
- Significance: Revolutionized Arabic calligraphy with measured and balanced scripts like Naskh and Thuluth, setting the standard for Qur'anic writing.
- Ibn al-Bawwab (d. 1022 CE)
- Works: The Chester Beatty Qur'an.
- Significance: Pioneered the use of Naskh script for Qur'anic manuscripts, making them more accessible. His innovations in spacing and alignment influenced generations of calligraphers.
- Yaqut al-Musta'simi (13th Century)
- Contributions: Refinement of Naskh and Thuluth scripts.
- Significance: Introduced the oblique-cut pen, standardizing calligraphic strokes and influencing Ottoman and Persian calligraphy.
- Ottoman Calligraphy (15th Century Onward)
- Contributions: Introduction of Diwani and Diwani Jali scripts.
- Significance: Developed for royal decrees and ornamental use, these scripts demonstrate the Ottomans' commitment to elevating Arabic calligraphy.
- Islamic Geometric Patterns and Illumination
- Significance: Integral to Islamic art, geometric designs reflect mathematical sophistication and an understanding of proportion, symmetry, and harmony. These patterns adorned mosques, manuscripts, and palaces, symbolizing the infinite nature of Allah.
- Gutas, Dimitri. (2001). *Greek Thought, Arabic Culture: The Graeco-Arabic Translation Movement in Baghdad and Early Abbasid Society*. London: Routledge.**
- Meyerhof, Max. (1935). "Ibn al-Nafis and His Theory of the Lesser Circulation." *The Isis Journal*, 23(1), 100-120.**
- Max Meyerhof was among the first modern scholars to rediscover Ibn al-Nafis' works on pulmonary circulation.
- Haddad, Sami. (1978). *The Physician Ibn al-Nafis, His Contribution to the Theory of Circulation*. Beirut: American University of Beirut Press.**

Bibliography

- Rahman, H. U. (1984). *A Chronology of Islamic Medicine*. Karachi: Hamdard Foundation.**

- Nader, Elisha. (1995). "The Rediscovery of Ibn al-Nafis' Manuscripts." *Islamic Studies Quarterly*, 18(3), 245-260.**

- Ullmann, Manfred. (1978). *Islamic Medicine*. Edinburgh: Edinburgh University Press.**

- Pormann, Peter E., and Emilie Savage-Smith. (2007). *Medieval Islamic Medicine*. Edinburgh: Edinburgh University Press.**

- Siraisi, Nancy G. (1997). *Avicenna in Renaissance Italy: The Canon and Medical Teaching in Italian Universities*. Princeton: Princeton University Press.**

- Nasr, Seyyed Hossein. (2006). *Science and Civilization in Islam*. Harvard: Harvard University Press.**

  Khan, M. Y. (2009). "The Life and Works of Ibn al-Nafis." Journal of Islamic Medicine*, 12(2), 56-75.**

- Hourani, Albert. (1991). *A History of the Arab Peoples*. Cambridge: Harvard University Press.**

- Rosenthal, Franz. (1992). *The Classical Heritage in Islam*. London: Routledge.**

- Al-Masudi, Abu al-Hasan. (c. 889 CE). Muruj al-Dhahab wa Ma'adin al-Jawhar (The Meadows of Gold and Mines of Gems).

- Al-Idrisi, Muhammad. (1154). Tabula Rogeriana (The Book of Roger).

- Al-Idrisi, Muhammad. (1154). Nuzhat al-Mushtaq fi Ikhtiraq al-Afaq (The Pleasure of Him Who Longs to Cross the Horizons).

- Lewis, Bernard. (1993). Islam and the Discovery of the West. Oxford: Oxford University Press.

- Harley, J.B., and David Woodward. (1987). The History of Cartography, Volume 2: Cartography in the Traditional Islamic and South Asian Societies. Chicago: University of Chicago Press.

- Ahmad, S. Maqbul. (1960). "Cartography of al-Sharif al-Idrisi." Islamic Culture, 34(3), 171-182.

- Sezgin, Fuat. (2005). Science and Technology in Islam, Volume 2: Astronomy, Geography, and Navigation. Frankfurt: Institute for the History of Arabic-Islamic Science.

- Burnett, Charles. (2001). Arabic into Latin: The Reception of Arabic Science in Europe. London: Routledge.

- Nasr, Seyyed Hossein. (2006). Science and Civilization in Islam. Cambridge: Harvard University Press.

- Rosenthal, Franz. (1975). The Classical Heritage in Islam. Berkeley: University of California Press.

- Toomer, Gerald. (1996). "Al-Idrisi and Medieval European Geography." Journal of Historical Geography, 22(2), 123-140.

- Kennedy, Hugh. (2004). When Baghdad Ruled the Muslim World: The Rise and Fall of Islam's Greatest Dynasty. Cambridge: Da Capo Press.

Printed in Dunstable, United Kingdom